CREATING UTOPIA

Suzy Bootz

Creating Utopia. Copyright © 2016 Suzy Bootz. Printed and bound in the United States of America. All rights reserved. No part of this book may be reproduced or transmitted in any form or by any means, electronic or mechanical, including photocopying, recording, or by an information storage and retrieval system – except by a reviewer who may quote brief passages in a review to be printed in a magazine, newspaper, or on the Web – without permission in writing from the publisher. For information, please send email inquiry to info@suzybootz.com.

Although the author and the publisher have made every effort to ensure the accuracy and completeness of information contained in this book, we assume no responsibility for errors, inaccuracies, omissions, or any inconsistencies contained herein. Any slights of people, places, or organizations and unintentional.

First Printing 2016

ISBN: 978-0-692-64801-8

ATTENTION CORPORATIONS, UNIVERSITIES, COLLEGES, AND PROFESSIONAL ORGANIZATIONS: Quantity discounts are available on bulk purchases of this book for educational, gift purposes, or as premiums for increasing magazine subscriptions or renewals. Special book or book excerpts can also be created to fit specific needs. For information, please contact suzy@suzybootz.com

TABLE OF CONTENTS

The Reason 7
Interview with author Suzy Bootz 9
Introduction 13
Identifying Illusion and Fear 21
Discovering Your Purpose & Living Your Passion 29
Creating Utopia 41
What Color is Your Faith? 47
The Courage to Paint Outside of the Box 55
Being More than One-Dimensional 63
Write Your Story 69
You Are Chosen 77
The Intersection of Illusion and Utopia 85
The Dream Walk-Through 93
Create a New Normal 99
Facing Your Fears 105
The Illusion of Time and Separation 113
Whispers from Heaven 119
What Will You Contribute? 129
Joy is not a Destination 135
Reflections of Grace 141
Discovering Your Truth 149
Connecting through the Veil 157
Being in Alignment 165
I See You 173
It Isn't About the Money 179
Wherever You Go, There You Are 185

Accepting Your Purpose 191

You are the Creator and the Observer 197

Hope vs. Faith..205

Being One with Your Destiny 211

Write Your Story..219

The Lottery Illusion 227

Stay the Course 233

THE REASON

Prayer has always been very sacred to me, and I can remember as a child knowing that part of my role in prayer was to speak to God then wait for a response. When I felt God was speaking to me, I could hear the words echoing through my soul. This book is filled with the words that echoed through my soul when I dropped to my knees one afternoon and asked God to show me my truth. Throughout this book, the Source, also referred to as God is that perfect and all-powerful spirit or being that I believe guides us all. Source is used throughout this book to describe this spirit or being, because this transcends any man inspired religion. These words are only *my perception* to the answer to *my* prayer through the communication I have established with my Source energy. These words are not meant to replace any doctor's advice or any other necessary treatment. They are merely a documentation of the answer to my prayer, in hopes that they will inspire another person to seek Source energy from within their soul.

INTERVIEW WITH AUTHOR SUZY BOOTZ

Question: Suzy, why did you write this book?

Suzy: I began writing this because I felt in my heart I was at a point in my life where I was truly at a standstill. I was scared. I left a job that I had a career in for about 17 years, and I had started becoming self-employed as a pageant coach. I really felt in my heart I needed some clarity, and in order for me to get clarity in my life I have found that writing is the best tool for me and the best instrument for me to be able to do that.

Question: Are these your words in a conversation you are having with God?

Suzy: They are. I have always believed in the power of prayer. As a very young child I can remember having talks with God and hearing His voice in the echoes of my soul. This was the way I was able to process all of the information that was coming to me, because I literally dropped to my knees one afternoon. I was so scared and so upset, I said God you have to show me my truth and suddenly I felt the strongest urge to write. It's these words that I had been familiar with, the way they filled my soul that began to coming through to me. I knew that this was my prayer being answered by God, it was my conversation with God.

Question: In the book it does seem like you are often talking about your life, but it also seems like you're talking about *my* life, about anybody's life.

Suzy: Absolutely! The amazing thing about this was, ever since I was a little girl I felt in my heart I was going to have a "calling" to inspire somebody. I knew through inspiration that it would be through a connection with God. He is literally within each and every one of us whether we acknowledge this or not. As I became more aware of the words that were flowing through me, they were relating to my questions and to my fears but they were also words and instruction that could guide anybody. As I wrote these words the most amazing feeling came over me. Every time I would sit down to write, I felt connected to God and through these messages I not only felt the words come through me but I really felt the emotion and the love that God was expressing to me about His love for all of us because we are all connected. We are all one.

Question: Well, then let's hear what you and God have to say.

"What some consider luck as they witness the manifestation of another's dream is seldom understood for truth, which is the love and passion this soul used to create that which the world seeks to label as luck. If you dismiss the creation of abundance with another's luck, then you disregard the absolute truth that you can create what your heart truly desires through self-love, self-acceptance, and self-sufficiency. My child, you have witnessed this truth in the world around you, and have seen many fall from their own grace. You are about to unfold a truth so deep, that this dream journey will be written in order for all who seek the truth of their own existence to understand. They will not doubt that they too have the power to turn thought into abundance of that which brings them joy."

Excerpt from Through the Eyes of Truth:
A Conversation with God about My Life, Your Life, and
Discovering Our Purpose

INTRODUCTION

What would you do if you heard the voice of God speak to you? Would you recognize the voice of Source or would you disregard it as the voice of your own imagination? As someone who believes in God and the power of prayer, I heard God whisper into my soul a very specific message. "I want you to document your dream journey, so others will be inspired by your truth and realize they are never alone. I hear their thoughts, I know their voice, and I feel their cries." What if God spoke those words into your soul and asked you to write your journey so others could be inspired by the power of prayer? What would you do? How would you respond? Would you answer the call?

This question seems so simple yet God whispers into *your* soul every day. How did you respond? What would you say when God asks you to believe in a dream so great that the world around you would consider it luck? If God says to you, "I want you to trust me. Trust me to the extent that you believe in the power of your dreams before they are even realized. Do you have the faith to do this?" How will you respond when you hear the voice of truth resonating within the walls of your soul, asking you to step up and own your faith? What if God asked you to believe in the message you were receiving to the extent that you had to write your prayer journal out word for word? Only then the world would look back at your journey and realize they must look within to hear the voice of their own truth.

Every day we are called upon to trust the voice of God yet we doubt that voice which we hear is actually Source energy. We are more willing to believe that others heard us reaching out to them through an email or a telephone call, yet are less willing to believe that God, our own Source of life, heard our call. Why? At what point in our life did we learn to disregard the voice of truth for the voice of fear? When were we so willing to acknowledge our own fear and illusion and convince ourselves of something that isn't real? As children of God we are born into the truth that our connection with our Creator is the most important relationship we can have. Yet as we grow into adults we learn to adopt the voices of fear in order to be accepted by the world around us who is worshiping illusion.

What if God has been speaking truth into your soul for years and rather than disregard the message, you listened. Really listened to the answers to your prayers. What would your life be like if you learned to silence the noise from the world outside of you, and tune into the sound of Gods voice resonating through the walls of your soul? I learned to tap into the voice of God and wrote my first book titled "Through the Eyes of Truth – A conversation with God about My Life, Your Life, and Discovering our Purpose." The words were literally the answer to my prayer when I asked God to show me my truth and help me to discover my purpose.

What happened from that moment on was that God showed me my truth by revealing to me my passion and my purpose. I learned that my passion was writing, just as it had been since I was in the third grade. I felt very connected to something greater than myself when I would put pen to paper. I discovered my purpose when God revealed to me through my passion of writing, that my purpose was to connect you to God by reminding you that we are never alone. God loves us more than we can ever imagine, and we never actually die but pass on from the physical to the energetic level. You could say that I discovered my purpose through my love for writing.

Have you ever asked yourself what your purpose is in life? Better yet, when was the last time you asked God a question and waited long enough to hear the answer? If you knew that every prayer you prayed was felt, heard and acknowledged, would you pray more and listen longer? This takes not only shifting your attention within, but getting comfortable in your own soul and establishing a relationship with God. This relationship also takes the faith to believe in your calling and the courage to walk the path alone. Are you ready to do this? I asked myself this question before I began every book I have ever written… and especially this book.

God spoke into my heart several years ago that I would be documenting my dream journey so others would not only believe in the power of prayer, but once again believe in the power of God. This dream journey began when I lost my mother in 2004 and I had to understand on a soul level the truth that we are all connected. Once we pass on from our physical body, our souls are still very much alive. Even though we can no longer see or be with our loved ones once they pass away, we are still very much loved by them, comforted by them, and reminded by them that this life is just an illusion.

The reality lies within the walls of our soul where we are connected to Source energy through the oneness that is life. We have never been apart from God except through our illusion of being separate from Source. Once we change our perception and realize the power of our dreams are within us, then we realize the connection we have to the miracle of life. My miracle of life encourages me to write and live out my purpose with a grateful heart and an open mind.

These pages were my introduction to Creating Utopia, a place where all is perfect and where miracles happen. Now I am going to leave the rest of these pages to be filled with my answered prayer. You see, in my quest to enjoy my love for writing I learned that God connects to me when I connect to God. So when I continually heard God whisper into my soul to begin my dream journal I knew it was time. Creating Utopia is about creating love and connecting to a place within where the experience of love, joy, and peace is created. All I have to do is just connect to "utopia" within my soul instead of looking for it in the world outside of me. I believe that Inside of all of us lies something that is our own soul imprint. We can't learn it from the world outside of us, but instead remember it from the world within us.

Utopia represents life, love, and endless opportunities. For me it represents a place to call home, but not necessarily the home which is built from bricks and mortar. Rather the home that resides within our souls where every dream is a possibility and where we are all one with God. Where we are all one with each other through the power of God whether we are in the physical or spiritual realm. This is my story and it will be filled with the pages of my life that are deliberately created to share with you how dreams are created through the power of prayer and faith. Utopia is love. Utopia is life everlasting. Utopia is oneness where we are all experiencing ourselves as a part of the greater whole. This is only my perception of how dreams are created when God whispers into our soul and asks us to answer the call. I believe that God speaks to us throughout our moments, yet we are so consumed with the world around us that we fail to hear His voice.

Sometimes miracles need to be created in order to awaken us out of our trance and remind us that we can write the story of our own lives through the hand of God. Each of us have the power to create miracles in our lives. We only need to remember that we are not defined by our circumstances, rather by our Creator. Abundance is not for the special or lucky...abundance is our birthright. So I ask you again, what would you do if God whispered into your soul and asked you to answer the call? Your journey is only one prayer away.

"Whatever your heart and soul seeks in love, ask God and it shall be given unto you. For you are all extensions of Source energy, and cannot be separate from love except for your perception of the separateness. Seek that which your soul wishes to experience in love, and you will witness your world flow abundantly in love."

Excerpt from Through the Eyes of Truth:
A Conversation with God about My Life, Your Life, and
Discovering Our Purpose

Lesson One
IDENTIFYING ILLUSION AND FEAR

"When one soul awakens to the reality of its own perfection, a light is magnified that lights up another souls awakening. The tide of love is beyond measure. For you and I are one, and I am one with every soul you encounter. Thus in your awakening, your energy awakens another from their illusion."

Excerpt from Through the Eyes of Truth: A Conversation with God about My Life, Your Life, and Discovering Our Purpose

My child there is a blanket of fear that has covered the hearts of many souls. This is why you have answered your call. To remind another soul that reality lies within them and not outside of them. People need something to believe in. Whether it's a sports team, a celebrity, or an author reminding them of their own greatness, the souls in this world need to believe in themselves once again. What often occurs is these beautiful souls who are inspiring the world are not giving credit to what is the source of their truth, which is their Source. So many attempt at all costs to convince the world that they are the Source of knowledge, truth and success. Because so many have learned that reality lies outside of them, they create fear from the theatre of their own minds.

So many of you have convinced yourself of the illusion that you owe yourself to the world, because you believe they have given you what little you have. So in this creative process you choose to convince yourself of a lie. That somehow you as a child of God, a co-creator in your own destiny you owe yourself to the illusion of another. You choose to relinquish your own dreams so another may step on your path of greatness. You choose to walk away from your destiny in order for another to create it as their own, and yet you wonder why it is that you are sitting in the dust of that which could have been.

My child you have convinced yourself that you know not the blueprint of your own soul and yet blame me for not correcting your steps. I can lead you to the river of life but through free will you must desire to walk through it, and open your eyes to the truth you have been avoiding for so many years. Somehow you convinced yourself you are without power to think for yourself and create your own destiny. When you lost your sense of identity is when you chose to adopt the illusion of thinking that another taught you. Why are you in such denial of self when you know from the depths of your soul that which you are trying to create first begins within the walls of your own kingdom?

Why would you attempt to continue creating fear in your own life by walking a path that is built on the bricks of fear and illusion alone? You know truth from within your own heart yet you seek it outside of you and wonder why you see it not. For you cannot continue denying self and wondering why the world you have created within is not reflected in your world without. It is from the untruths you have adopted the illusion that the experiences which you seek are still rooted in fear. If it were love and truth you were seeking, then you would remain within the walls of your own soul and continue connecting to it until you realized it in the world outside of you.

Even as you write these words you have connected to that source of fear instilled within you so long ago. You cherish your dreams so deeply that you have convinced yourself of the illusion that you will not give them away to the world around you. This is why you have chosen to only see a part of your greater whole my child. For in one moment when you felt your dreams crushed from the hands of another, you imparted the fear within your blueprint so deeply that it became ingrained in your creative process. Now you must realize this fear was illusion. As quickly as you made the decision to create your life from this illusion of fear, you can disconnect from it and release it. This no longer serves you.

Choosing to protect yourself by *not* creating love in your life is deliberately creating fear in your life through your own hands. Do you not realize the moment you allow yourself forgiveness for relinquishing your dreams to another, is the moment you release judgment and allow yourself permission to accept your own gifts? You need not the approval from another to receive that which you have already created within the power of your own mind. The pain experienced from loss of any kind often lingers in your heart and mind. Since your creative process is born from thought and emotions, then the pain you have yet to release becomes a part of your future creations.

Now is the time to forgive self and to realize there is nothing you can create from your world within that another can take from you without your permission. For you once granted your dreams to be gifted to another. Yet what you failed to realize was if it was truly your passion then you would have held it for only yourself to experience. These dreams you have stored in the corners of your mind are being created from love and for honoring your purpose. It does no soul any good if you continue creating your life from fear. Cease from looking at the world outside of self for direction when they are seeking to discover their own truth. Instead look within for guidance and I will lead you to your truth.

Utopia is a state of mind my child, much like being in a state of peace and love and this begins and ends within the soul. Ask yourself if there was one dream you could create today, what would that dream be like? For I have instilled within each of you a blueprint so authentic that only you have the power and the passion to create it from the inside out. What would you create today if you knew your miracle needed only to survive on your thoughts, emotions, and actions? I tell you this my child, your soul can no longer deceive itself by looking at the world outside and calling it truth. You know what your creative energy has made, and soon the world will discover theirs as well by seeking guidance from within.

What would you dream if you knew you could create anything from the power of your own mind? Create something so magical that the world around you would call it a miracle if they knew you brought this creation into being, specifically for them to remember their own greatness. You have discovered your passion for writing and your purpose for reminding others they too have the power to create anything they desire through thought, love, and action. Your dream would include empowering another soul would it not? Create something so big that another soul would know they too possess the same creative power within their own soul. Remind them through the creation of your own dreams, that all they need to do to bring more love into their lives is go within and seek first the kingdom of God.

As you identify your fears, your dream becomes an even greater possibility. For it is already alive within you and has been seeking you as much as you have been seeking it. There is nothing you can do to separate yourself from your greatest vision except through your own perception of not having it. Alter your perspective and the world around you will appear different than it has before. Identify your fears and understand by holding on to that which brings fear and anxiety into your heart, you alone are keeping the fear alive. You must change your perspective, and realize the familiar emotions of fear prevent the new emotions of love from uniting as one.

Just as you have understood that you and I are one, we have always been and will forever be one. Yet when you lose sight of your truth you feel separate from me. Your dreams and greatest visions are no different because they all begin and end with your perception of illusion or reality. The illusion is that you must seek your dreams in a world outside of you, when in fact the reality is your dream has already been created. You need to see it and feel it alive *within*, and your world outside of you will reflect the world within you. For I have shown you visions and prepared you for your calling in such a manner that you have in fact created utopia, and it seeks you in a way greater than you can imagine.

Everything needed to be aligned to form this blessed place, this state of mind that allows you to appreciate yourself as a co-creator in your life with me, your Source energy. You needed to write these words in order to understand how the creative process works. More importantly you needed to realize that you need only to connect to God within you to create a magnificent world outside of you. As you have documented your prayer to me, you also now document the creation of your dream so another soul may understand their own greatness. Stop seeking approval and guidance from a world so lost, they no longer remember who they are. Realize your thoughts are creative energy seeking to connect with the desires of your own heart. Only when you align with love on the deepest level will you know what is yours and how it came to be.

For you need not worry about doing, rather be in a state of just being. Then you will recognize your soul whispering itself back to you from the echoes of your own heart. You will never create your greatest visions by focusing on a world of lack. As you reach for your truth within then you will gain a better understanding of reality. You create your own opportunities from your thoughts and recognize them when they present themselves to you. So many souls in the world today seek to claim something that has never been theirs to begin with. They spend countless hours, days, and years claiming they are deserving of something they never created. When they fail to take from another that which they felt entitled to, they blame God for not having it. Had they actually sought me from within and connected to their truth, they too would realize their greatest dreams becoming a reality.

Instead these same souls will blame me for their inability to recognize the truth of their own existence. They cannot claim that which another has created from the depths of their own souls. It comes not down to the love of God for one soul being greater than another. For I am one with all souls and love each and every one of you greater than you love yourselves. Why would I pick and choose what soul is allowed to experience their own greatness while another sits back and wonders why they too are not favored? The souls in the world around you who are accomplishing dreams are those same souls who sought the creative process from within, by connecting to their love and purpose through the power of God. They need not explain to another soul why they received that which they alone created. For the creative process takes courage and faith to pursue. Every soul who is experiencing life in the physical journey is creating. Whether they are creating a life built from the foundation of fear or the foundation of love, all souls are creating their journey.

Would it not serve you to understand the creative process so you can choose to create a life of love? Denying yourself your greatest gift only keeps you in a state of fear. Change your perception of truth and realize that anything you desire to experience begins within your soul. Then it becomes manifested in the physical world around you. You need not explain to another why you are worthy to create a magnificent life if they choose to see the world through the eyes of limits and fear. You need only accept that each soul has the power and the choice to create in the manner which they desire at any given time.

The holidays are soon coming and once again you will witness many souls standing in lines for a sale item, and focusing on obtaining material possessions which in time will no longer serve them. These souls believe they need something outside of themselves in order to feel complete. They spend such little time within the comfort of their own souls. So they would rather live in a world where lack and fear is the prominent emotion, than take the time to seek truth within their own souls. I have reached these souls and reminded them in many ways they need not the material things of an illusion filled world. Their greatest gifts lie unopened within the walls of their own souls, and if you only knew what you are capable of creating you would spend less time in these lines and more time in solitude connecting to your greatness.

Only then when you choose to stand in lines for a sale item that you desire, will you do it for the enjoyment rather than for the need. You have trained your mind to copy what you witness in the world around you then convince yourself that is all you can create. Imagine a world where less time was spent watching televisions and computers, and more time was dedicated to living a life of purpose. Can you imagine what you would each accomplish and how happy and filled with joy your lives would be? There would be less lack and more abundance in all areas of life you desired to experience. Instead, you witness the world around you creating lack and you convince yourself the only way to have, is to take something you never created to begin with.

You witness souls in the world around you being recognized for achievement and consider them the lucky few, when in fact you are as lucky as they are. The only difference is your perception of what you believe you are capable of. One soul who wins a lottery is no luckier than the soul who lives in lack and misery. As co-creators with God and children of the all mighty, abundance is every soul's birthright. The difference is the soul you witness winning wealth or a new home has connected to their abundance by going within and creating it from the inside out. Yet too few of you realize this truth, so you continue living your life convinced of an illusion that I favor one soul over another.

It is you who favors to live a life of fear rather than love because so many of you have grown used to experiencing those feelings. The possibility of feeling a different emotion of love and gratitude is so foreign to you, that you would rather continue experiencing more fear. Change the way you think and feel, and your world around you will change as a reflection of that which you have created. Go forth and choose one thought of love over an old thought of fear, and you will grow more comfortable experiencing love. You are all born of love and are connected to love through Source energy. I am with you always and will be a part of your love story forever.

Lesson Two
DISCOVERING YOUR PURPOSE & LIVING YOUR PASSION

"As you deny yourself, you still deny me, and once again deny the purpose of that which you were created to perform. Own it and accept it through the grace that I have bestowed upon you. I have called you forth my child not to adhere to the worlds fear, but to accept and receive my love."

*Excerpt from **Through the Eyes of Truth: A Conversation with God about My Life, Your Life, and Discovering Our Purpose***

Within each soul lies a blueprint so authentic that nobody else can recreate it as their own. This blueprint celebrates your passion and the journey your soul has taken to discover itself as a co-creator with Source. Your journey unfolds into pure love and potential when you connect with your blueprint and understand that it too searches to connect with you. Knowing this, you can no longer deceive yourself into an illusion you must seek that purpose in a world outside of you. When you discover your purpose and live your life on the path your journey is meant to take you, only then will you realize that utopia has been within you all along. Your state of being is meant to bring you peace and love and celebrate all that you are.

Cease from searching for your truth in a world filled with illusion and fear. Look within your own soul to uncover your treasures of knowledge and love which overflow in abundance. My child you have searched your heart and realized your gifts lie within your spirit to connect you to me, your Source of love and inspiration. Can you imagine a world where every soul would seek their truth from within and live their purpose with no regard from another's approval? Your purpose has always been to empower souls through prayer and their intuitive gifts. Yet you realized many years ago this purpose could not be sought from the world outside of you. So you ceased from chasing illusions and began honoring the signs your soul was providing you along the way.

It has taken you many years to acknowledge your own gifts lie within your ability to create inspiration through the power of your fingertips. Yet because you had been programmed from a young age to seek your truth from the world outside of you, you perceived the world through one set of lenses. Rather than realizing your blueprint allowed you to create your life story in a unique and colorful manner, you attempted to fit it into a box created by another. Now you understand this blueprint calls not only for your courage to move forward without indication of evidence seen, but calls for your faith to trust the process by which it takes.

Since your purpose is to connect souls to the truth of God and through answered prayers, you also understand that as you are one with your Creator you are one with another. For you learned from the death of your mother that souls continue to live on far beyond the constraints of their physical body. When you trusted your intuition, you wrote a book about the perfection of life after the physical body. Although prayer and life after death appear to be separate for you they are actually very much the same. For your connection to me through perception of oneness creates the connection of love and perfection. Your awareness of oneness with those whom you loved and have crossed through the veil of light also become alive through your perception.

Each of you are connected to one another through the truth of me, your Creator. If you choose to view one another as separate, then you choose to disconnect yourself from the Source of love and light. How can you view yourself as one with me when you perceive one another as being separate from me? If you embrace the truth that I am one with every soul living in the physical body and in the energetic state of vibration, then how can you perceive separateness with these souls? It contradicts the truth that you and I are one, as I am one with every soul as well. Your words and the power of truth you are experiencing comes from the depth of a purpose so authentic, you desire to share it with another who may be experiencing the pain of loss. Seeing every soul as one with their Creator and every soul as one with you, allows you to bring hope to the heart of the broken who have yet to see beyond their emotional pain.

Your words will stir within another a truth so deep that they will become aware of the love that connects them to another and ultimately to me. By writing the love story between you and your dream, you allow another soul to look beyond the physical and see their world of truth through endless possibilities. This is why your purpose has taken you to this journey through life my child. You can see that which lies beyond the walls of illusion because your journey through prayer has opened your mind, your heart, and your soul to the unlimited possibilities where dreams become reality, and life exists beyond what the eyes can see. Is this not a beautiful story to share with another when it comes to manifesting their dreams?

Since you have renovated several homes, I will explain this in a way of thinking in the same manner which is familiar to you.

When you renovate an older home in which you desire to freshen up and have it reflect your life in the manner in which it is today, you must see beyond the walls and boundaries once created by another. Your mind must have a vision in place that sees beyond what lies in front of your physical eyes so you can see the end from the beginning. Changing your perception from focusing on what currently is to what becomes possible, creates opportunities to challenge your mind to create a sanctuary that reflects your life. Even though the old walls prevented light from shining into a particular room, you can knock those walls down to create a room filled with more light.

See your mind in the same manner as you would envision a renovation project in a house. In order to create a new sanctuary that allows you to have all you desire, you must replace the old with the new. As you review each room of the house, you decide through deliberate thought what you desire the new structure to look like and how that new design will make you feel. Already you see that you are creating from thought and emotion, and the action follows when you tear down the old walls and replace them with new rooms, brighter lighting, and vibrant color. You see the world of unlimited possibilities when you realize this structure can be renovated any way you desire to create it. Room by room you begin to replace the old with the new, until you realize the entire house has been transformed to reflect that which brings you love and joy.

You understand you must replace anything that needed to be repaired in order not to bring old problems back into your new structure. Your way of thinking is much the same. In order to only create that which you desire to experience you must be deliberate in your thinking, know the emotions you desire to create, and replace the broken things in need of repair with new experiences of love and joy. One would never imagine to keep old leaks and problems and bring them into a newly renovated structure. You know if the problem is not rectified then you will bring the same old issues into your newly renovated home. Yet so many of you choose to change your physical features through diets and new clothing without changing the interior, which is the strength of your foundation. You keep the same old negative patterns of thinking, which bring in the same experiences of fear into your life. Once you rebuild on a weak foundation then the house becomes compromised, and you will continue to create more of the same old issues until they too are repaired.

Rather than just changing the appearance of your life, go within and see your life as a newly renovated foundation which can support your passions and purpose. Bring new light into the old and darkened rooms of your soul where your dreams were once hidden in fear. Take each room that housed your dreams and seek the blueprint of your new sanctuary which represents your life. No longer choose to support old habits of thought that bring in the same uncomfortable fears and anxiety. Instead you can choose to deliberately support the new vision of your life through allowing air in a once stagnant room of hope into your soul. Tear down the walls you built from attempting to convince yourself of an illusion that never existed.

For your dreams that lie dormant in the rooms of your soul are calling to you through the echoes of my whispers into your heart. Rather than ignoring these dreams, choose instead to honor them by answering their call to you. It takes you more energy denying self than it would to honor your soul calling. Seek your kingdom of heaven within and you will see the transformation of your world outside of you my child. I love you greater than you can imagine yet by turning your attention from your truth, you turn your attention away from me. For your truth resides within your soul where I am waiting to help you nourish and love yourself and honor your calling.

You need not seek the attention or the approval from a world outside of you, for you will never receive the permission to love self from another who has not yet called their soul home. They will only serve to convince you of an illusion they have adopted. This being that you are not worthy enough, powerful enough, or magnificent enough to create the life of your dreams. Rather than reading another person's story as they create their lives, choose instead to write your own and claim your deepest desires from within. You have already created that which you desire to experience my precious child. If you just turn your attention to that which you desire to see I tell you this, you will see it form before your very eyes.

What has happened instead is the world which you create from fear thus creates more fear. Rather than noticing things in your life for which to be grateful for, instead you focus on seeing those experiences built from fear. The only reason you choose not to see truth is because you are more comfortable creating fear as it is all you know. Learn to become comfortable being uncomfortable, and you will notice your transition of comfort changing into love. You must learn to first become comfortable in the stillness of your own thoughts and remove judgment from yourself. Once you do this, you will grow to be in solitude through your silence and as you close your ears to the noise of the world around you, then you will hear my voice echoing in the stillness of your heart.

So many of you convince yourselves the reason you no longer pray is because you believe that I no longer hear you. My child it is you who chooses to no longer hear me. If you believe me not, then take a look at the house in which you live which is your body. Many of you feel betrayed by your own body yet refuse to take responsibility for that which you have created. If you are living a life of love then you should be comfortable sitting alone in a room and listening to the silence of your own soul. This house where your soul resides is where you decide what enters through your doors, how you express your passions through living your purpose, and ultimately how safe and serene you feel once in it. If you cannot be alone in silence with self then how do you expect to quiet your soul long enough to hear God speak to you?

For when you pray you seek communion with Source and you must be still in the silence of your soul in order to hear me answer you. The more uncomfortable you are being alone with self, the more you resist the opportunity to hear my voice. My child there has never been a moment during any point of your existence when you were separate from me. It is through your own perception of self when you feel uncomfortable being one with me. As the more you judge yourself for not being perfect or worthy enough to be in my presence, the less you allow yourself to be present with me. This is a gift that you have complete control over, and yet you blame me for not wanting to be present with you.

My child it is time to awaken to the truth of your illusion filled life. You spend so much energy attempting to believe in something your soul knows is not truth. What you choose not to realize is that every moment you are awake, you have an opportunity to create oneness with your God. Yet what happens is you choose not to be alone in silence to hear the sounds of my voice echoing through the walls of your soul. Having the chance to create a new life every moment you are awakened will allow you to recreate your life as you desire to experience. What this entails is you being deliberate with your thoughts and creating from intention instead of reaction. Just as a builder renovates an existing house that they desire to recreate, every detail is planned out in every corner of the rooms to ensure the plans reflect the perfect outcome.

Consider yourself your house and greatest sanctuary. Once you go within to each room of your home it must reflect comfort, love, and peace so you can feel safe and harmonious. In order create this sanctuary you must be deliberate in knowing what you desire to experience and how you are going to control the details of your renovation so you can feel at home in every inch of your house. Can you take charge of every detail of your life that you have the power to control and be deliberate in your creation? Instead of living your life through repetition and a trance-like state of mind, are you willing to change your thoughts and recreate your life to represent it in every detail that brings you more love and peace?

It begins with the intention and the power of the mind can create what the world would consider to be a miracle. What they fail to realize is the power you have to create your miracle lies within each and every soul. You have only to desire the change and be deliberate in choosing your thoughts to reflect the emotion of love you are seeking to experience and your actions will follow your mind. Since you created your thought patterns through repetition then you must recreate them through repetition as well.

In order for this task not to appear to overwhelming then look at your house or kingdom having many rooms. In these rooms lie your hopes, fears, desires, and your purpose. Take one room at a time and clean out the room of fears by realizing that whatever caused your fears no longer exists in the present moment. What often keeps your fears alive is the attention to pay to the memory which recreates the experience and the focus of the emotion the incident created. Prayer will be a part of your process so you can begin to see your life through the power of being a co-creator with God. Take each room and one by one choose to renovate it in the detail you wish to experience it in.

If your room which holds your dreams seems vague and unclear then clean out the old limiting thoughts and illusions you chose to adopt from another and only fill that room of dreams with my truth. That being you are a child of God and have the ability to create any dream you desire. The only difference between not having created your dream and living it in the moment comes down to the choice of perception. If you have closed the doors on your greatest dreams, then open your mind and heart to the creation of them and acknowledge there is something great within each of you that only your soul blueprint will create. There is no need to compete in a world outside of you for something you already possess within you. The only difference is choosing to see your world through the eyes of truth rather than illusion.

Now is the time to empty out what no longer serves your spirit and live in peace. Open your windows of possibilities to the truth that you already possess that which you desire to experience. By connecting to self within and discovering the power of communion with Source, you allow yourself glimpses of your blueprint to begin revealing itself to you once again. Now you will be open to receiving this blueprint in love rather than avoiding it in fear. My child there is nothing you cannot have if you first create it within, in order to see it manifested in your world outside of self. You must be connected to your dream in such love that you dedicate yourself to spending time every day in the creative process.

Put your computers down and cease from spending your lives obsessed with another person's life when you have the power to create a magnificent life of your own. You need not be born into wealth or fame to create beauty in all that you do. You have only to seek me within you and there you will build on our relationship. Can you imagine a world where every soul is living their passion and walking their purpose? There would be so much love radiating that utopia would be present more than fear. You must realize in order to create your greatest vision for the world it must first begin with self. The power you have to create lies within yourself and since you cannot control another soul, the person who ignites the change you desire to see in the world is in fact you.

Fear not that you may be walking this path alone, for as you and I are one I can never be separate from you. For I am your greatest guidance system and the Source of all that is. How can you perceive your journey into self as being lonely and frightening when in fact I am one residing within you and experiencing a part of the whole through you? With any dream journey you have a responsibility to seek truth and guidance from within. As you are an authentic child of God, you have come into this journey through life with a blueprint you created from love. You need not seek that blueprint or purpose from anyone outside of you. For who knows on a soul level what road is the best path to take if they know not your blueprint?

As you journey into communion with your Creator, you will see more clearly the path you are to take and you will replace fear with courage and faith. Are you prepared to walk this path with me, your Source of love and life? I seek only to support your endeavors and lead you back to a heart that is filled with wonder and appreciation for life. Fear not that the road will be frightening, as you cannot deny yourself anymore. There is nothing more frightening to a soul than to separate from their Creator and walk a path of illusion alone. This is what you have been doing for so long my child, so realize you have only to enjoy the journey as one with me. For I love you greater than you can imagine. Allow my words to echo through your soul and choose to build your foundation of love that will bring ripples of more love into your life. I love you now and forever.

Lesson Three
CREATING UTOPIA

"Lastly, you must be aware that love and time co-exist, so if you are spending your time creating that which you love, you will in turn create the life of your dreams. That my child, is the secret of life that so many souls have been seeking."

Excerpt from Through the Eyes of Truth: A Conversation with God about My Life, Your Life, and Discovering Our Purpose

What is it you desire to create my child? What dream do you have that lies so deep within your heart, you need to seek it before you believe it seeks you as well? For the moment you realize your creation of a peaceful state of mind lies within, then you become full co-creators of your universe. So many of you seek to establish your dreams by first seeking that which has already been created outside of you. Yet what you fail to realize is that you cannot claim something outside of you that you have yet to create within yourself first. Why then do so many souls choose to seek illusion from the world outside of self when they have yet to understand how the creative process came to be?

Souls in this illusion are more willing to convince themselves they are entitled to own the vision of another without first creating it. Every day through perceived competition, so many of you go to work and fight for attention, praise, and power. You then get home and fight for the attention of your loved ones and your time. Yet so few of you are willing to relinquish the illusion of competition. Realize attaining anything you desire must first begin within your own mind. Take for instance the perception of luck. What you see when you witness the realization of another's dream is often mistaken for luck. Even though someone may have won a contest at the local convenience store or millions of dollars in a national contest drawing, the perception is much different than the reality.

For as you witness another soul create a lucky win, the perception is their name was randomly drawn from a selection of other's and by pure chance were able to receive their prize. The truth is, this particular soul created the experience of having their name drawn far before the drawing ever occurred. For if you desire to experience anything you love, you must first create the emotion and connect the thought to already possessing that very thing you desire. It takes more than one moment of thought to create a pattern of manifesting. As your thoughts connect with your internal power, the focused energy is what brings it to form.

Yet you spend so many hours and years creating patterns of those experiences you no longer desire to have in your reality through your repetition of focused thoughts and emotions. I want you to challenge yourself and create that very experience you desire to connect to in your physical journey. What do you need to do in order to bring that very experience into physical form? As you have discovered my child, all your creative power lies within you so the prayer of asking for the experience you desire is setting the intention. From there you are connecting to your greatest Source of all that is… your Creator.

Realizing you desire the ultimate experience of the emotion of love allows you to focus your attention on that which you love. If you desire to create a dream house and have it not in your physical experience, then realize your dream house first resides within the walls of your soul. Envision the beautifully lit rooms in every area of your soul and walk through the doors of these rooms to experience those emotions they will bring you. For these rooms represent not only borders for which to place your belongings. They represent emotions of love when you have family walk through the passages that connect you to something greater than yourself. You can experience those emotions now. As you visualize the colors every room will have and the emotion you experience within the walls of these rooms you experience this very moment in the creation process.

What will your writing room look like as you sit down and watch the waves of water from your beautiful room? While envisioning yourself creating words from thought, what emotions do you experience now as you visualize the sound of water hitting the wooden decks? What color is the sunset you witness every day as you sip on a cup of your favorite tea and connect with your soul mate sharing the moments of your day? Do you feel the breeze as you are sitting on your new sundeck and soaking in the warmth of the sun? What are you praying to me as you feel in gratitude of your new house?

What about the large and serene pool that allows you to enjoy the water you so much love any time of the day or evening? As you embrace the light pouring into your new kitchen as you welcome a new day, do your feel more empowered by your creative energy? Every room in your sanctuary represents beauty to you, and what is more astounding is that you created these very colors in your mind before the architecture of this house even began. They represent the colors of the ocean my child, and the colors of your faith.

For as you sit in these rooms and walk through your dream home, you remember the colors of your heritage and the emotions of both the joy and love they represent to you. Even as a child in a Caribbean country where you once began, your journey to empowering souls through reminding them of their truth was already stirring within you. Even though you felt emotionally broken when losing your precious mother in this physical journey to cancer, you brought a part of her spirit through the vibrant colors on these walls. Her role in empowering you and placing the truth of your value before your eyes was the conduit you needed to fill your role as a personal development coach.

As you learned your commitment to self began through self-love and self-respect, you built your books and your lessons on the foundation that all of your dreams begin within your body and not as a result of your body. What a precious lesson to teach all souls, especially those young women who represent a lost world outside of them. For each of you have a purpose to light the world one word and one thought at a time. Your journey was to help spread awareness that beauty shines from your thoughts and power from your own heart. You need not compromise yourself for another in order to feel loved.

All you need to do is go within self and enjoy the journey you created one page at a time. My precious child, you search for yourself in a world that is a complete illusion and wonder why you fail to discover your purpose. I have witnessed so many souls lose dreams, hope, and self through their journey because somewhere along the way, the believed a false illusion. Someone convinced you that you are defined by your beauty and empowered only by another. Yet how can that be when every soul is made in my likeness? Would I not then create all souls to be equal in their own creative capacities? Would I not create women and men to have the same power to design a life where they are living their purpose and inspiring the world around them to do the same?

Yet so many of you create your life through copying those experiences created by another. As a result, you adopt the illusion that their way is the only way to create. You have chosen to impart knowledge to souls who wish to be reminded that their own greatness lies within the walls of their soul. What better way to do this than to reveal to those who wish to be reminded of their own greatness through the power of courage and an act of faith. As you uncover the creative process of your own soul, you share with others the slightest possibility that you can create your deepest desires through extraordinary achievements.

These need not be the patterns that others choose to create their lives by or share their passions through. As you write you create a memory of patterns you forgot so long ago when you too convinced yourself of something that was not truth. Even though you once believed your worth would come from the hands of others, you have transitioned to empowering those around you by creating unique approaches to thoughts so many have. You must ask yourself each moment of creation if you are creating your life by design through the power of being a co-creator in your life. Or are you creating the same experiences each and every day whether they bring you love or fear.

This role you chose to play in the storybook of your life allowed you to remind one more soul they too have the power to create from thought and emotion. Instead of looking at the world outside of you and claiming a "prize" that was never yours to begin with, you chose to share your dream journal in hopes that another will seek their dream from within. This is the song every heart wishes to experience my child. You have so much power to create a life of love through so many moments of your existence, yet you get lost in a world outside of you that supports not your dreams.

Creating utopia is creating a state of presence where you are experiencing divine love and joy. Each of you have your own utopia within your soul, and in this physical journey is where you are called to enjoy the passions of your heart and live out the purpose which brings you more emotions of love. In the journey you will inspire another to seek their own greatness through the reflection of what you have reminded them to be. Is that not a purpose worthy of every soul who crosses into the world of illusion for moments of time?

Set aside any preconceived notions you may have once believed and seek truth within your own heart. There I will guide you to the waters of life where you will experience so much joy in living out your purpose. Through this passion you will inspire others to seek truth through prayer and knowledge through the power of God. Be still and know the time has come to welcome into your life the glory of my presence within you. For all who see this transition of truth will wonder where they too can create from a place so majestic. When they seek me with an open and humble heart, I will connect them to a world where miracles are the norm and love is unconditional within and outside of them. That my child is what you would consider to be utopia.

Lesson Four
WHAT COLOR IS YOUR FAITH?

"Have faith that you already are what you have dreamt of becoming. You already are that which you are attempting to be. As your plans pave the road for others to travel, you will soon realize that the prize was in the journey all along."

Excerpt from Through the Eyes of Truth:
A Conversation with God about My Life, Your Life, and
Discovering Our Purpose

Believe. This is such a powerful word, yet how often is it used throughout your moments in this journey through life? You insist you can create miracles from faith, yet so many of you lack belief in your dream, in yourself, and in your co-creator. Faith. It is the key ingredient from turning your visions into tangible goals throughout your life, yet because you must discover this within you it becomes more difficult to develop. Somewhere throughout your life you stopped believing in your own ability to validate your talents and use your gifts to bless yourself and the world around you. Why? Have you become so consumed by your insecurities that you refuse to honor your own life in the precious moments you are blessed with? How is it you believe in the dreams of another enough to spend your waking moments consumed with rising to meet their standards and neglect your own passions?

Belief plays a role in your creation of both reality and illusion. You need to harness your faith in order to enjoy your talents and experience self-love from them in this journey through illusion.

You also need to believe in what you cannot see, which is in truth your reality. What you think about you create, so your world in essence is created from your beliefs. Ask yourself what you believe at this moment in your life? Better yet, your life does not lie so look at the world which you have created and there you will witness the evidence of your belief system. Are you living in a world where you are supported in love from those around you? Has your journey through life taken you through roads that have been less traveled or are you hanging with the rest of the "pack" to create the same life they are creating?

You challenge those around you to seek a world where they need not the support of others, yet you have created your world in illusion and fear. If you don't agree, then ask yourself why you have to place yourself in a continual environment of denying self and experiencing your own gifts. When you awaken in the morning, are you happy to start your day by giving thanks for your gifts and your life? Or are you waking up in the morning, depressed and anxious about what lies ahead of you? Have you painted a picture of colors that you can enjoy throughout the day and use your talents for self-expression, or are you stuck in an illusion of fear where each day you spend your time doing the same job with the same people who make you miserable? What color are you painting your moments with? Are you creating your life from the same monotone colors that have been passed down to you from your parents and generations before them?

Every day you get to choose what you desire to create in your life, yet so often you experience the same situations that create the same feelings you had the day before. Yet rather than question this creative process, you become anxious and more fearful because you think you are stuck in this self-imposed environment. If you would only stop briefly and realize your choices are what create the world in which you live. Granted you cannot control the world around you, but you can control your own thoughts, emotions, and actions that create your reality. Rather than worry about how you can manage your emotions in a difficult situation that does not serve your greater good, change your focus to thoughts that create new experiences for you.

Ask yourself what color your desire to paint your self-expression in your reality at this moment. Rather than using the same colors that brought you fear and sorrow, choose something new. If you desire to experience a world where you are filled with joy, then what do you have within yourself today that will allow you the experience of joy? What untapped gifts can you use to manifest new emotions that will create new experiences for you?

As children you are taught the world is filled with possibilities. Even in your youngest years you are taught that you can paint your life through pages in colors that reflect your greatest joy. As you grow into adulthood, you create self-imposed barriers so you convince yourself the world is no longer filled with possibilities. Instead you force yourself to believe an illusion that colors no longer exist, and the world must be created just as others around you have created their world of illusion. Somehow along your journey you forget what you were once taught as a child when you saw your world through the eyes of endless possibilities. You forgot to use your own imagination to paint your pages in the story of your life through colors that reflect your deepest passion and your greatest sense of self-expression.

For so many years you convinced yourself of an illusion, that you forgot what truth is. You alone get to create your experience through this journey in life using the colors that you desire to create. If your passion represents the colors of the rainbow, then use those colors to create new hues and allow your greatest expression of self to be told in the pages of your life. Stop repeating your life from patterns that no longer serve you seize your greatest expression of self in this very instant. Choose your thoughts wisely and let them be the greatest reflection of who you are today, not who you once were or worse yet, were told you had to become.

If you allow yourself to create your life experience using only colors and thoughts that represent what you love, then you will create more love and more experiences in which to love. So much of your lives are wasted just going through the motions of what you believe you are supposed to do. Until one day you realize it is too late to take those moments back and retrace your steps in the creative process. Do you not understand my child, the act of creation involves you being aware and deliberate in your process? If you continue to choose to create your life from a trance, then you will realize your life is unfulfilled. Yet by changing the course of your life through new habits, you can once again take control of your experiences and live your life through passion and love.

What color of the rainbow is your life course on today, and realizing you can change your patterns then how are you going to paint your life now? What do you choose to do and to think in order to create the experience of love in your life? If you love to paint yet have chosen not to make time to live your passion, then what are you going to do now to bring love through painting into your life? If your desire is to use your hands to create art, or your feet to run and enjoy fitness, then how are you going to incorporate these passions into your life today?

You must believe in your own right to honor your soul journey and live your life in the manner in which you were created to live it. As co-creators in this journey through life, you need to cease from creating your moments with those lost souls in the world around you. Instead choose to seek truth within and there you will find me. Waiting and loving you through the depths of your own soul, and just seeking to experience self through being a co-creator with you. I will show you colors that you have never even imagined as you harness your talents and share your gifts with me. When you do this, I will honor you by reflecting back to you in the mirror of life what a magnificent creator you are. Never again seek to justify your talents and your gifts from the world around you. The intention of your life was to express yourself as a co-creator by using your own passions to ignite the light within your own soul.

In order to do this you must believe you are worthy of experiencing a life so great that you need not seek the approval from the masses in order to be great. Since you are experiencing your greatness through the expression of your gifts, then believe you alone are the soul who is meant to enjoy the nourishment of your own talents. Once you approve of self by honoring your spirit calling, then you will create more situations in which to express your higher self. Never again attempt to stifle your creative growth by diminishing your talents. For you are all in this experience of illusion to discover new ways to create the expression of you. Without the faith to honor your gifts, then you will not have the courage to paint your rainbow for yourself. So ask yourself, what color is your faith?

What do you wish to create for the fulfillment of your own soul? How do you desire to review your moments when you are called home and have only the movie of your life to play out before you? Will you cherish the life moments, or will you view them through the eyes of sorrow and regret? My child there is no greater regret than to stand at the doorway in the veil of light and witness your moments pass by you on the screen of life through the eyes of sorrow. Throughout their lives so many souls long only to be true to self. Only when they pass on from illusion through the veil of light do they realize the wasted moments they spent trying to fit into another's illusion.

My child, the greatest gift you can give to self is to accomplish that which your soul seeks to discover. For through the moments of creation when you are manifesting love in greater waves than you can imagine, you understand the journey your soul seeks to uncover. There is no greater illusion than fear, and so many of you create your lives in a state of continual fear. To the point that you fear shifting your soul from that fear into truth and love. Yet I send you countless souls to remind you that you are not alone in your journey. Their goal through moments in their journey was to help you lift the veil of illusion and see the world through the eyes of truth.

How is it my child that you desire to remain in a place of fear because you have grown so accustomed to it that it has become your new normal? Yet your loved ones who you have mourned for because they have crossed over before you, desire nothing more than to help you discover your truth before you are living in your world of spirit. Although their greatest regrets have been to live their physical lives through truth, they love you so much that they desire to remind you to enjoy your moments now. Live your life now through the eyes of truth and the heart of love. Then when your moment comes to cross over on the wings of Angels, you are more joyous than your heart will know.

Cease from viewing the illusions of the world around you from a place of fear and see it for what it is. The representation of your truth reflecting back to you, only desiring that you awaken from your trance and take control of your vehicle called life. No longer choose to sit back and wait for life to happen to you. Instead, step up to the road of life and realize you are the author and the story. You are the journey's beginning and the story's end. There is no such thing as sitting back and waiting for the world around you to grant you permission to live. Rather you are the driving force in your life. Realize you are the only soul who you need to seek approval from whether or not you are granted permission to experience your greatest self from the world outside of you.

What color is your faith as you seek to know your soul through your expression of self? Do you wish to paint your days with vibrant colors of love as you deepen your relationship with Source and with self? Every day you stare at a blank canvas called your life. When you awaken in the morning, rather than seeking to express yourself through colors that reflect your deepest desires, you paint the same gray as the day before. As a result you experience the same emotions and thoughts, leading you to duplicate the same actions day after day. Your life should represent passion and purpose through all you do. If it does not reflect these things then discover the change waiting within you. All you have to do is change your perspective to design your life with the colors that create passion. Begin today to do this and you will discover emotions of love and joy so deep within you, your life will never be the same again.

Lesson Five
THE COURAGE TO PAINT OUTSIDE OF THE BOX

"When you finally hear the voice of truth resonating from your souls, have the courage to act upon it. Grace is not a gift that is blessed only to the wealthy, but to those who love and respect the glory of their soul's truth. You are all such perfect and worthy souls, and my gift to you is for you to recognize your perfection within your lifetime and celebrate it. ."

Excerpt from Through the Eyes of Truth: A Conversation with God about My Life, Your Life, and Discovering Our Purpose

Seek the expression of your soul from the comfort of knowing that which is truth cannot be denied except by you – the creator. Understanding this will allow you the freedom to express your true purpose and live out your life journey, by creating experiences that only support that purpose. So many of you will go to your resting spot and cross through the veil of light denying yourself your greatest gift. The gift of self-love is one that cannot be gifted by another, yet so often you seek this love outside of yourself. Why? When did you become convinced of an illusion that it is more important to love another more than you love yourself? Further yet, why would you consciously choose to deny yourself of your greatest soul gifts and then blame another for your lack of happiness?

Do you not understand the greatest form of love one can give is to share your heart and soul with yourself on this journey through life? The more you reach within the walls of your own soul, the greater you will discover our connection and my hand reaching out to you as well. For you are co-creating your life with me and as a co-creator, you are not separate from me. Seek the authenticity of your soul expression through embracing your unique and colorful soul. Rather than attempt to fit into a certain mold that the world outside of you perceives to be you, allow yourself to shine from the inside out. You need not seek the definition of your blueprint by looking to others to define you.

Yet all too often this is what you wait for. A sign or token of affection from another person who you deem greater than yourself. You starve for your own soul to embrace self, all while seeking approval from the world without to grant you permission to express yourself. Your greatest dreams and your deepest visions of self-expression are waiting to be embraced by you. Can you imagine how your soul will dance during every step of your life when you grant yourself the permission to experience your purpose? This is why you look at the world around you and see the lost gaze in so many people's eyes. You have denied yourselves for so many years, you no longer know who you are.

You have allowed the world outside of you to tell you what to feel, how to should act, and what to think. Every step in your journey has been to walk for another, that it becomes obvious why you spend the rest of your life journey on autopilot. Your minds become numb to your own heart, that the mere thought of seeking self within is too difficult to bear. You have chosen to travel many years in this trance and now you are awakening out of your sleep to a calling that has been stirring within your soul for many years. Yet rather than acknowledge it as your truth, you sought approval from the world around you. Only you discovered that nobody understood your calling enough to endorse it.

Do you really believe as a co-creator with God in this journey through life, your role was to seek the approval from the masses to become your greatest self? You bow your head to me yet close your heart to my response. The truth lies within your own ability to create your experiences through free will. For my role in your journey through this illusion of life was never to override your decisions, rather to support you while you were in the process of remembering who you are. You are a child of God and all you seek to create through love lies within your own soul. Tune out the voices of the masses around you who have been struggling to embrace their own perfection, and listen to my whispers echoing through your soul.

Do you wish to write the songs of love that will someday bring a woman to tears on her wedding day? Then sit down and write that song. There is no such thing as tomorrow. For time is an illusion yet you treat it as the master of your destiny. If you wish to paint a picture that evokes the greatest essence of your soul, then take the brush in hand and use your free will of choice to create that masterpiece. For you need not the approval from the world around you to exercise the power of creation you are born with. If dancing is your gift to yourself, then stand up and move your body to the fullest expression of who you are, not who the world desires for you to be.

When you walk past a basketball court and refuse to dribble the ball because you fear what others around you will think, then you deny your own soul's desire to create love in your life. When you dismiss your dream of someday becoming a great teacher and giving a child a chance for a better life because you believed in them greater than they believe in themselves, then you once again deny self. If you witness the grace of a soul walk across a stage and dance to the beat of her own heart as she shares her passion with the world, and tell yourself you are somehow inferior to this dream, then you deny self. For who outside of you is to instruct you on becoming the greatest version of yourself, if they are not privy to the passion and purpose your heart is calling out for you to create?

Yet all this time I sit in wonder and awe of you, a co-creator with me and ask why you are not seeking truth from your Creator? You pray to me in the still of your moments when you recognize the spark of life within your own soul. Yet as quickly as you ignited your dream you choose to cover it with a dark blanket because you fear the world outside of you will not approve. Where is it written in the book of life that your greatest dreams are to be approved by the masses? Better yet, where is it written in the creative part of your soul blueprint that you are to be supported by another soul who has yet to understand their own greatness? Yet look at your life and ask yourself what visions of greatness you have hidden in the walls of your soul because another person failed to applaud you for sharing your authentic self?

You dreamers are ridiculed for desiring to create greatness from the power of your own soul only because you demand the approval from the world around you. Look around you and ask yourself who you know that has created a life so filled with love and joy that you desire to mirror that life by following their choices. Yet when you accept the ridicule and pessimism of another soul, you have in fact chosen to create the life they have chosen to create. So few of you are walking through life living your own purpose and seeking your greatest potential from within. You are too busy sharing with the world around you the superficiality of your soul that you don't even know who you are.

Ask yourself this very moment who you are and what you represent. If you cannot answer this question posed to self, then now is the time to seek your truth from within and stop looking outside of yourself for your definition of self. So few of you can share a simple explanation of who you are, that you prefer to tell others what you want. Who you are and what you desire are two completely different things. Who you are as a co-creator in life and as a person who is filled with love for everyone but yourself is not the same as what you desire. For who you are is a perfect child of God, experiencing self through an illusion called the physical world. What you desire is often the outcome of your own soul's neglect.

Learn to discover who you are so when you meet a stranger you desire to share self with, they become a compliment to you rather than a need. Their role in life is not to fill your cup, as you have all you need to fill your own cup. Yet because you fail to understand self, you seek to have others define you through the only mirror they know…the mirror of their own experiences. So many of you beautiful souls have painted yourself into a tiny box that does not remotely represent who you are. Remember you are co-creators in life. If you are not deliberately creating experiences that reflect your own greatness, then you are creating your life through an illusion. More than likely you are creating your life through the illusion that another has convinced you is your reality, when in truth it is theirs.

When you pray to me, ask that truth be revealed if you no longer know yourself and your own greatness. My child I will reveal a truth so encouraging that you will desire to only seek the expression of self before you ever seek it from the world around you. Learning to remember who you are and what you are capable of will allow you to see yourself and your ability to create a life filled with greater love for self. Suddenly you will see your world reflected back to you in colors that represent your passion and your soul calling. If they are colors you have never painted before, then be the first to paint them. No longer worry if you are coloring in the box you were told to paint. Instead choose to paint outside the box where you get to define the miracle of creation.

Each of you have the ability to create such beauty and joy in your own lives, and if you would only seek truth of self from within then you would discover yourself the way I see you. If you could only see your glory through the illusion you have chosen to create, you would never spend another day wasting time and energy painting in the same box you were taught to paint your life in as a child. You would magnify the glory I have given you by celebrating your soul which is where you will discover your purpose. You were never created to become an imitation of one another. Instead, you are all called to discover your own unique gifts and use those gifts to bring more love and joy into your own lives. Only then will you cease from seeking your glory in a world outside of you.

When you make the decision to be true to yourself, then you will understand the power you have to create your dreams from mere thought. No longer will you question you own ability, but thrive on the internal search of your heart to bring your imagination to light. What are you going to do this very moment to create the color of your soul in your experience of life? Instead of seeking approval through self-posted photos on the internet, seek to acknowledge your own soul and the creative power you have to make any dream a reality. For I am with you every moment of your lifetime, so why not call upon me to be your Source of inspiration in your life?

Lesson Six
BEING MORE THAN ONE-DIMENSIONAL

"The walls that create the rooms within the house must also be built for a reason, which is to house the different areas that make the house unique and special with its features. These walls are sometimes built because one wants to shut out a dark corner and store things that no longer serve their greater good, and these walls need to come down one by one. As they come down, you can replace them with new walls that allow the doors to open into the adjacent rooms that store the wonderful gifts that create love in your home. Look at your life and how you can improve the construction of your temple, and you will always seek to improve yourself in ways that will bring more love and light into your house."

Excerpt from Heaven Scent:
Love Letters from Beyond

How are you defining yourself when you experience your moments on your journey through life? You must have an idea of your own ideals, otherwise you are walking through your waking moments in a trance and just existing instead of living. Do you see how important it is my child to define yourself and the road you wish to travel? So many moments I watch you in awe of the creative and perfect soul that you are, and wonder at what point you will awaken from your trance and see yourself through the eyes of truth. You live in an illusion and rather than create your moments through the world of abundance, you strive to be the person you see reflected back at you from the mirror of the world.

Do you not wish for something greater to fulfill your purpose than to spend your days attempting to be average and blend in with your environment? You fear becoming average, yet I tell you the greatest fear you have is being masterful. For you have convinced yourself of an illusion that in order to be accepted, you must be average. Rather than striving to live your own life through tapping into your world within, you seek to blend in and not be noticed by the world around you. Why are you so frightened of living your life to suit your purpose? Have you not yet realized those who become frightened of their own greatness lash out to you not because you dared to achieve your purpose? They lash out at you because they fail to achieve their own. You are serving as a mirror to the world around you.

Rather than devote so much time and energy attempting to become invisible, why not use your resources to connect with Source within you? I will show you a way so complete that your soul will ignite a passion that changes the way you perceive life and the world around you. Choose not to be subservient to a world of lost souls who declare their own greatness while hiding in the safety of illusion. You are all far too great to be stifling your own growth, yet you do this each and every day that you choose not to live your purpose and create a life of passion. You each have such power within your souls to create a life that allows you to awaken in the mornings and be in gratitude for all you have.

Yet instead of choosing to create your own life by design, you hide behind the curtain of illusion and fear. Wondering when you will get your chance at experiencing your own greatness. I tell you this my child. With every decision you make to hide behind the illusion of another's power over you, your light becomes dimmer. Make a decision on this very day to live your life through your own passions and step out of the illusion of the box you have painted yourself into. Being one-dimensional and creating your life to serve another is not part of your journey as a co-creator. Yet know that as a divine soul who has free will to create your life as you choose, there is no right or wrong decision. There is however, a road you choose that will either take you down the path of love and joy, or fear and illusion.

The problem arises when you see the world around you as reality and the world within you as an illusion. There is no justice served in the creation of your life by playing small. When you choose to see the world for what it is, then your perspective opens up new opportunities that were always there just waiting to be recognized by you. Realize you are the soul who has placed yourself in the self-imposed limitations to your own greatness, and you are the soul who can break those chains. How? By seeing your life in a new dimension and painting the picture of your story with the colors you choose to create from the tools of your own self-expression.

Reality is such a magnificent state of mind because it affords you the peace and the comfort of knowing life is yours to create. Your self-expression allows you to empower yourself as a co-creator with me, and to realize your own creative capability. What a wondrous and beautiful place to be! For when you choose to view your own life through the eyes of truth, you will discover a new world of creativity waiting for you. Remove your fog covered lenses and see that you are capable of anything you desire to experience my child. You create experiences every day that support your illusion of fear or your reality of love.

What do you choose to witness in your world of possibilities now? When you step out of the fog of illusion you stand at the center of a world of possibilities. These include being as multi-dimensional as you desire to be! If your dream is to write poems, reach children, and tap dance to express your love of self, then you have the right and the ability to do all of these things. If you love expressing your creative talents through education, athletics, and performance then allow yourself to be as expressive as you desire. For your role as co-creators in this lifetime is to celebrate the song in your heart through all of your creative abilities.

There are no rules when it comes to self-expression outside of those rules you choose to obey. However keep in mind that many of these "rules" have been created by others who lived their lives in fear, and these rules are meant to keep you in fear. For if you choose to take the advice of another who has created their life from limitations and self-imposed boundaries, then you will create what they have created. Always be diligent about learning from others but be the seeker of your own truth. Refuse to believe in another person's illusion and most importantly, choose not to create your own life from those illusions. For as you have learned, fear creates more fear and love creates more of that to love.

If another soul attempts to give you advice on what is acceptable in the world in which you create your experiences, then ask yourself if by heeding that advice you are giving up a piece of your own soul. There always has to be the first soul who grants another permission to sing the glory of their own song, by staying true to themselves. Are you willing to be that soul who inspires those around you to seek their destiny from within? Or will you be another of so many souls before you who have created a life from fear and a foundation of mistrust to their own perfection? As creative beings of light in your life, you create through thought, emotion, and action. What you think about you create, so if you choose to think as another soul who has not created a life of purpose, then you too risk not creating purpose in your life?

Honor yourself and respect the short illusion of time you are granted to create your journey. For one day when you least expect it, you too will join me when you cross through the veil of light. Will your thoughts turn to regret of time spent being in fear of your own greatness, or will you embrace the journey because you had the courage to dance the song of your soul with all of your might? You are the composer in your life and you are the song my child. There is never a moment that you are separate from me, so there is nothing to fear by walking your path alone. You need not the permission of another to light your own soul through honoring your calling, so choose to be the voice you hear in a world where others are shouting to be heard.

As a child of God every form of abundance is your birthright, so cease from trying to convince the world around you that you are worthy. For you are the only soul to convince that you deserve to have all the experiences that bring you love and joy. Once you realize the truth of your own perfection, there is only creation to experience. If you desire to express love of self by painting, writing, running, playing cards, or walking along a beach then take time every day to do those things. You did not come into this experience of life to serve another person's illusion nor to limit your creativity. For you and I are one and together we experience life through you, so stop trying so hard to do that which brings you no joy.

Create a balance in your life by honoring your calling and you will reap abundance of joy. As energy beings you create from pure energy, so choose to create experiences that bring your soul self-love. Cease from seeking love from the world outside of you. As you grow more in connection with self and thus with

Source, you tap into a well of unlimited love and joy. This will you be able to share with those around you rather than seeking to take it from another. My child, you were born into this illusion equipped with all that you need to create a life of love and joy. However in order to do this, you must know what makes you joyous.

The color white is known of being void of color and holds the magnificence of all the majestic light frequencies. If you view your world in which you have created as being without color and representing all of the vibrations of hues, then allow yourself to be unique and paint yourself with the brush of the color you desire. No longer be willing to hide behind the sameness of those around you. Instead, you can shine your unique energy of light into the universe and allow yourself the freedom of expression through that which you love. My child, go forth into the story of your life and write out the pages as if no rules existed in the creative process. You have the ability to paint in colors you never even imagined. All you have to do is take the risk and trust Source within you. I love you my precious child and am with you always.

Lesson Seven
WRITE YOUR STORY

"Every soul on this earth has a beautiful "love story" in which to share their truth. Inspire the world by reminding them of this truth. When they are ready to seek me with all of their heart, they will come into a deeper understanding and knowingness."

Excerpt from Through the Eyes of Truth:
A Conversation with God about My Life, Your Life, and Discovering Our Purpose

Living in the moment during your life is one of the greatest gifts you can bestow to yourself. As so many of you waste precious time thinking about the worries of tomorrow, you create fear in those moments that are yet to pass. Rather than pondering the possibilities of fear in your future moments, choose to spend those moments in the actual creation of your life now. Live in the moment and allow your life to be your message. Consider yourself the pen in which you write the pages of your life in your book of life. Worry not that you have no message to share. What if your greatest message was to live life in the present moment and refuse to squander away those precious gifts you take for granted?

Instead of wondering whether or not you deserve to experience those things that bring you great joy, discover them through living out your moments. Whether you love to run, write, or create art, choose to do those things rather than just thinking about them. You are so careless in your moments of creation thinking about a time and place that doesn't exist, rather than embracing the time you have now to just do those things which bring joy to your heart. Define what your passions are by experiencing life rather than sitting back and watching life happen to you. Realize my precious child that you are the message of your life and you are the intended recipient of that message.

For if you have a valuable message in which to share with self through discovering self-love, should you not be the intended soul who that message was shared with? If you desire to run a marathon, then grab a pair of tennis shoes and move your feet one step at a time until you are experiencing the love of pushing yourself beyond your own self-imposed limiting thoughts. If you desire to experience swimming and the freedom from which it brings to your body, then do that which your body and soul desire to experience.

 You are so worried about pleasing another soul who has their own issues of self-love, you deny self the experiencing of living life to the fullest. Maybe the person who your story is intended to influence is actually yourself. Write the story of your life page by page, as you live your life day by day in the fullest capacity. When you realize there is no one but self to impress then you allow yourself such a freedom of expression through living your own life. Suddenly your attention shifts from watching to doing, and from wishing to having all that you desire. Not because you are suddenly rich with wealth, but abundant in self-love and respect for self. Ask yourself what daily rituals you desire to experience that you have yet to allow yourself to perform.

For your life was never intended to be placed in the corner of your own mind while you watch another person live their own. You spend so many hours in front of the television and the internet that you no longer know yourself. As you study the celebrities and those souls who have learned to master their own life, you neglect to notice yourself. As a result, one day you look in the mirror and don't even know who you are anymore. Do you think this is where your energy was designed to be when you came into this journey through life as a co-creator with God? I tell you this, you are wasting away your moments of authenticity when you choose to sit back and wait for your life to happen to you.

As energetic souls experiencing life in this physical journey, you escape your freedom of will every day when you choose to neglect your own desires and place them on the back shelf for another. Where is it written that you are experiencing your life journey to please another? Yet so many of you waste your talents and your gifts because you have not the confidence to just live your life without the approval from another. Each of you are all perfect souls having an imperfect physical experience in this journey through life. You are not in this illusion to be perfect, rather to live your own life purpose through creating love. For your life purpose is to create love through your own power of thought, emotion, and action.

Rather than beginning a new day creating the same old patterns, make a deliberate attempt to create your day by doing those things you love. You all have so much time, yet waste that time thinking about moments in your past or future that are not of the present. Then you lay in bed at night in emotions of frustration because you convinced yourself you have not the time to create happiness and a fulfilling life. Change your perspective to focus on self, and identify those gifts that are waiting to be experienced by you. These gifts will in fact create love and passion in your life because you love them. You honor them. You desire to create them in order to know as a co-creator in life, what it feels like to create love in your life.

Understand this my child and you will have tapped into a truth so powerful that you will never again seek love outside of self. Only when you learn to focus your attention within, will you realize that I am waiting to be the Source of love and inspiration in your life. No longer worry about whether or not another soul will approve of your passions, for you are not experiencing this physical journey to seek the approval of anyone outside of yourself. You chose to experience this life to cherish yourself as a child of God, and to know self through the freedom of your own creative energy. There is nothing to prove to another outside of you. There is only love to experience when you realize the power to love self is the greatest gift you can give.

So many souls seek a place outside of themselves where they believe will create an escape and an environment that will bring perfect love and peace into their lives. Yet what many of these perfect souls fail to acknowledge, is the love and peace they desire to know already lies within them. The only illusion is outside of self, for I reside within you as one with you. Seek to create a powerful connection to creation by seeking me within you. Only then will you uncover a journey that brings you such love and inspiration, you will know what it is to be alive for the very first time. You need not seek these things outside of you, for the only truth of your power lies within you. Realize the more you create self-love the more love you will have to share with self and with the world around you.

Your place of perfection lies not in the world outside of you, but in the world within you where I reside as one with you. Know this and deliberately create your life by this truth. Then you will understand the power you have from your very hands to create a life of purpose and passion. You will realize you need not the permission nor the approval from another in order to create a life of joy. Yet somewhere along your journey you convinced yourself of an illusion, that in order for you to achieve your own greatness by doing that which you love, you must first be acknowledged by another. If you love to sing, then you alone have the power to sing a melody anytime during your days and just experience the creation of song.

If running or dancing is your passion, then use the power of your healthy body to do that which brings you love and joy without seeking permission from another to experience this. Realize your body is a tool for expressing that which your soul desires to create in the physical realm. If only you could see yourself through the eyes of truth every moment of your existence you would never question your worthiness or ability to create again. You choose to see yourself through eyes of limitations or you choose to see yourself as an endless source of love and energy. Both of these perceptions are choices and they determine how you create the story of your life.

Would it not serve you to seek truth in prayer? There I will lead you to the waters of life and reveal to you that which you have forgotten when you chose to experience this journey. Your perfection as co-creators in life is to have all that your heart desires to experience. This is possible my child and the reality is waiting for you to walk through the doors of truth. Seek me within your soul and the answers to all knowledge will awaken your spirit. For within your truth are endless possibilities. Cease from writing your life through another soul's pen. You have within you all of the colors of the rainbow for which to paint your life story.

Just because one soul chooses to write their story through drama and emotional turmoil does not mean this is the only way to write. It only reflects their soul journey through this crossroad as they are finding their own way to self-love. Choose not to mimic another unless the story you wish to create is exactly as they are creating their lives. Chapter by chapter and word for word you seek knowledge by watching and imitating those around you, and wonder why you feel so empty and unfulfilled.

Your soul seeks the knowledge of truth through the expression of those gifts you came into being to share. If you choose not to share them with self then you choose not to share them with the world around you. Only by having the courage to write your life story word for word and be deliberate in your creation, will you recognize your own greatness awaiting you. Yet so often you choose to write the story of your life with the same words which create the same emotions and the same actions. If you were to review your life as it stands today, you would witness similar patterns of thought and actions. Yet you wonder why you stand before self in the reflection of your life and still feel the same frustrating experiences.

How can you not see the similarities of truth in the patterns that are creating your life today? Take a moment to read the pages you have already written and know just as you wrote out your life, you can change your thoughts and create newness in your life. You use the same creative process, except through deliberate intention you now create a new perspective in which to see self. As a child of God, I am here now and forever living as one within you. Lift the veil of illusion and see the grander vision that you and I wrote together before you entered this journey through the physical form.

Know as you see yourself through truth, your awareness of endless possibilities will also become evident to you. Those same possibilities will soar you through the ripples of a soul love so magnificent, you will lose sight of ever doubting yourself again. Are you prepared to take flight on a journey so deep, that it will not only transform the way you think but the way you feel about yourself and about God? Go forth and take notice of every word written and spoken from your power. Just as I have created from thought, emotion, and action through words so you will recognize your power to do the same. Live and soar in your light of truth my child.

Lesson Eight
YOU ARE CHOSEN

"To seek self-love, self-expression, and self-sufficiency is one of the greatest gifts you have chosen to experience. Now seek to know love and see all truth through the eyes of God, and you will create greater love than you ever thought possible."

Excerpt from Through the Eyes of Truth:
A Conversation with God about My Life, Your Life, and Discovering Our Purpose

Do you understand every soul on this journey through the physical form is experiencing their greatness? Yet rather than appreciating your differences so many judge yourselves and others for not being the same. You feel the connection of a dream so deep within your spirit, stirring and just waiting to be acknowledged by you. Rather than fostering it through love and building that dream within, you diminish its importance. You would rather betray self than to honor your calling because you fear the disapproval from another. Yet you wonder why so many of you are walking through this illusion of life feeling empty and unfulfilled.

If you spent the same time seeking understanding of self through communion with God as you do following another soul's journey on their dream, you would know what it is to truly be in co-creation with Source. Yet so many of you would rather sit back on the sideline of life and judge another for their co-creation and experiences, than risk being vulnerable and living your own life. You have somehow convinced yourself of an illusion that the world around you is your vision and therefore you are subject to the experiences presented to you. Choose to be proactive in your own life and understand that your dream will never be given to you by another. You must first create it from the power of your thoughts, emotions, and actions.

Knowing this, would it not serve you greater to actually seek truth from the depths of your soul and understand the power of your dreams lie not in the hands of another, but through the power within? Rather than looking at another soul who has accomplished a dream so great and wishing it to be yours, choose instead to seek the creation of your dream through prayer. If you spend energy and time wishing you too could have the dream another has created in their life, you may never know what it is to create your greatest vision. Instead of comparing the dream of another against your own worthiness, choose to value yourself enough to create your own dream.

You are all chosen to walk a path that is only yours to create. This path is made of cells and energy that only your soul can connect to. Within the course of this path is a dream so magnificent that you will awaken every morning to the anticipation of this journey. Your steps will align with its path and your heart will dance with every breath you take while enjoying your vision. You will feel so connected to me my child, this vision will appear to be a journey we are embarking on together. For the very first time you will know what it is to call your soul home and trust the answers to your prayers are being fed to you in such a clear and concise manner, there will be no doubt you are walking in your truth.

How is it then that instead of embracing this journey you fear it with all of your being? You are more willing to turn your back on your own soul rather than to have the courage to walk in greatness with God. Is it the approval from the world around you that you seek or the comfortable emotions of self-neglect and sorrow you are so attached to? If you fail to even question your own self-neglect, how can you understand that what you seek lies within you? My child you have walked on the road of illusion and fear for so long, you would rather remain comfortable being in the feelings of self-neglect and sorrow than risk walking a new road. Are you more in fear of your own greatness or is it fear of God that terrifies you?

As children you learn from those before you that God is an all-mighty force to be reckoned with if you step out of line. You are taught that if you choose to perform even the slightest "sin" you will be punished for all eternity. So you learn to fear me rather than embrace me. In the same breath of those who are sharing with you their versions of me, you are also told that if you ask for forgiveness then I will forgive you of such sin. How is it that you choose to adopt the illusions from another rather than seek your own relationship with me? For if you chose to seek communion with your Creator, you would embrace me rather than be in fear of me.

I tell you that you must learn to decipher your relationship with Source rather than adopt the relationship another has established with me. For if you choose from your own free will to live in an illusion of fear, then you will continue to create more fear. I ask you this. How can you discover your greatest vision of self without first seeking truth from within? How is it also that you must first choose to seek truth in prayer, yet have allowed yourself to fear me for so long that you do not pray? For if you are in fear of your God and know that I am residing with you, then you have not the courage to seek truth from within. Realize you and I are one and as you judge self, then you judge me. As you condemn self, then you condemn me. As you embrace and cherish self, then you embrace and cherish me.

For I am a mirror of you and am never separate from you. If you look at your life in the manner which you have created it today, are you satisfied with what you see? Are you waking in the mornings seeking truth and glory through your own hands, or are you condemning self to live out another person's vision? For as you judge self, you place limiting thoughts on your own potential and on the power I have to provide you the life of your greatest dreams. I have created you with a purpose to know self and become master of your own world. A world in which you can control how to create more love through the grace of your heart and through the power of your own hands.

Choose to seek your path through the words that resonate within the walls of your own soul. For you are a conduit for change my child, but the change you seek must first begin within yourself. The world outside of you is only a reflection of how you perceive yourself from the world within. When you realize your purpose is that of love and abundance of all you desire, then you will begin to deliberately create your life in love and abundance. You are chosen to create a path that is yours alone. It cannot be sought with the guidance and approval from the world around you. The desire you have, combined with the love in which you seek it will bring the road to your vision.

Suddenly doubt and fear will be removed and the illusion of fog will lift to reveal a path so extraordinary, you will revel in the journey with me. You will seek only truth from my guidance. Your fear will transform into courage to complete what your soul desired to create before your existence in the physical plane. My child you are becoming aware of your connection to truth, or you will not have traveled to this place now to discover Source as the conduit for the change.

Stop seeking your purpose in a world that reflects only illusion. Cease from comparing your calling to the calling of those around you. For as you are all experiencing life through the extension of me, you have not all desired to experience the same things. One may be co-creating their life in the world of abundance and wealth, while another is co-creating abundance and joy through relationships that are more valuable to them than silver and more priceless than gold. For if you would only cease from searching for your truth in a world outside of you, then you would understand your calling has a greater voice when you tune into it and just listen. What is your soul speaking to you when you shut out the noise of the world around you? What dreams are waiting to be manifested as they echo within the walls of your heart?

My child, you are chosen to create something so great by first discovering greatness within yourself. If you would realize your truth is as valuable as the recognition you seek from another, you would spend more time valuing yourself and honoring your inner voice. For that voice you wish to silence every day is in fact my voice speaking truth into your soul. Rather than seeking to escape it, choose to be still and listen. If I ask you to reveal to the world around you the vision of something greater than they are aware, is it not of interest to you to ask how? I will answer you and await your next co-creative move until together you and I have created that vision from the mere attention to it.

You must have the faith to see that which lies not before you in the physical form and the courage to act on it even though every seed of doubt is springing forth. You desire to reveal to the world the creation of utopia, but my child you are the one soul who seeks to understand. Courage is such a powerful emotion in which to act upon. For it represents to you the voice of truth in that which you have been seeking and the love of that which you desire to create. Walking alongside me one step at a time allows you, the creator of your greatest vision, to understand that which you are creating so you may share it with those who wish to know.

Creating a blissful and joyous state of mind is similar to creating a house on the sand which cannot be moved. The foundation represents the faith you have to add value to something that in the world's eyes has lost its value. The courage represents your ability to take action and tear down the walls to design a greater purpose for that structure. Finally the vision you have to see beyond the old walls and dingy rooms represent the ability to have a dream beyond that which the eyes can see. Dream your life through the eyes of truth my child and create your dream brick by brick so the foundation cannot be touched. For your dream represents the dreams of so many souls who desire to construct a vision to call their own but have forgotten their own greatness.

All too often a soul will witness the creation of another's dream and attempt to claim it in the name of Jesus. Yet what they fail to realize is this dream was in fact created through the power of the divine with the soul who created it. Why then would a soul think they have the right to claim something that was never theirs to begin with? The creation of this dream in which the souls of the world choose to claim was in fact created through the power of God and through the power of love. Why would I then grant them the creation of a dream another soul designed through the power of their own thoughts, emotions, and actions?

What these souls fail to realize is that when they witness a creation of something spectacular in the world of illusions around them, it is not the inception of that dream rather the result they see. For one or a group of souls have already created that which they see months or years ago. Once a dream is manifested for the world to see, you must understand one has already created it. Therefore there is not another who can lay claim to it. Yet so many of you fail to understand the creative process. You believe once a dream is in the physical world, it becomes fair game to another to lay claim upon. Then you lack communion and understanding of our relationship and ask me to bequeath it to you. Not understanding you too have the power to create a vision so magnificent that it lays dormant until you choose to bring it to life.

Then when you realize this dream will remain in the hands of the soul who created it, you question your worthiness and my love towards you. My child what you fail to understand in the creative process is the reality behind the illusion. For the manifestation of the dream you see was once a seed planted in the soul of the person who was chosen to create it. Yet what appeared to be my "choosing" your dream was in fact you creating it and planting it in your reality. You did this long before you even chose to enter through the veil of illusion and walk this physical journey of life.

As a co-creator with God you must realize the importance of discerning truth from falsehood and love from fear. For you know on a soul level whether that which you wish to "claim" from the hands of another is in fact yours. Yet you choose to convince yourself of the illusion that this particular dream is yours, when in fact you know on a soul level there is no connection of truth to your illusion. Rather than ask me in prayer what you are meant to discover in this journey, you blame your Creator for not allowing you to take another's manifestation of their chosen purpose. Somehow it becomes so much easier for you to convince yourself you have no control over your dreams than to take responsibility in the creation of your own life.

How does this serve you my child? Do you experience more love from keeping yourself in an illusion than you do by honoring your own voice? Now is the time to understand you are not the product of your dreams, rather your dreams are a product of you – their source energy. How then can you define your worthiness in my eyes through attaining a dream that you alone had the choice and the power to create? Do you now understand my child the difference between being a dream creator and a dreamer? One uses the power of your thoughts, emotions, and actions and the other watches on the sidelines of life and wonders why they feel unfulfilled. So I ask you my child... which one are you?

Lesson Nine
THE INTERSECTION OF ILLUSION AND UTOPIA

"Use not the illusions of time or lack in which to deny yourself any longer. I tell you this, through denying self, you are denying uplifting another. You are responsible for your own gifts. By sharing them with yourself, you share them in turn with the light of souls around you. Instead seek to fulfill a purpose greater than yourself. Look to Source within for the courage to guide you where you need to go."

Excerpt from Through the Eyes of Truth: A Conversation with God about My Life, Your Life, and Discovering Our Purpose

Before embarking on a journey in the physical form, you prepare yourself to know where you are going and how you plan to arrive. Whether you are walking to the kitchen in the morning to get your first cup of coffee or driving in a new city, you seldom just walk aimlessly around not having an idea of where you are going. Yet when I call unto you to seek truth and wisdom from within, you fail to respond in the same manner. You would rather seek direction in the world of illusion than to first discover where you are going in your spiritual journey for which you seek love and joy. How can you convince yourself these are two polar opposite journeys?

Would you not agree that the physical and the spiritual journey are one when you are in the vehicle of your physical body? Your body rarely embarks on a journey without your mind first navigating the safest and most direct and enjoyable route. Yet you would rather neglect your own soul than to risk listening to my whispers echoing throughout the walls of your truth. If you continue to follow your physical senses and convince yourself that is all there is, then you will continue to neglect your own soul and put your journey with me on autopilot.

My child you have come to the intersection where your illusion has met your truth. You are at the point of illusion and utopia, and must be deliberate in the direction you wish to continue your journey. As you stand at the crossroads of life you get to choose as to how you will co-create your life. Do you desire to create a life of love and joy from using your spiritual gifts and honoring your calling? Or would you prefer to continue navigating blindly down the path where many walk while having no loving direction or purpose? Your soul has brought you to this intersection so you can make a conscious choice as to how you are going to create the life of your dreams.

What do you choose? As I watch you stand in awe of the possibilities of your choices, I am still so connected to you, yet you fail to see me. You have forgotten that I have been a part of you since your inception. I will never be apart from you other than through your illusion of creating separateness. I plead to you my child to take notice of the signs I have given you that remind you of a journey you created so long ago. A journey only you can walk through faith and courage. Although I am very much a part of you, I cannot take control over your direction because we agreed you would have free will to create your life as you please. I honor this vow every moment I watch you create a life of fear. Now I desire only that you take notice of me and hear my voice echoing through the walls of your soul. Do you hear me?

Each of you beautiful souls have the power to create so much love and joy in your lives, yet rather than question your journey every day of your physical life you blame so much of your loneliness on the world around you. I witness you deceive yourselves and buy into the fear that you have minimal control over your own lives, and wonder why you seek not the truth through prayer. When you stop long enough to realize you are in essence walking around your spiritual story with your eyes closed tightly, then will you awaken to the possibility there is more than you are aware of. The same thoughts, emotions, and actions you have control over to take yourself to a job every day where you feel unfulfilled and lonely is the exact same process you use to create your deepest desires. The only difference is in your awareness of being co-creators with God.

How can you believe a falsehood that there is a difference in the creative process between creating a life filled with those experiences which bring you great love and those that fill your walls with fear? There is no difference in the creative process other than what you are thinking, feeling, and how you are acting in these moments of creation. There is absolutely no difference in the creative process between creating one dollar from thought than a million dollars. For all of it first begins within your mind, connects to your heart, and is followed through with your actions. Somewhere along your journey you have adopted a fear based illusion that prevented you from desiring the millions of dollars and somehow then blamed me, your Source energy for not having it.

My precious child this truth is something that you must realize before standing at the intersection of love and fear. So often you are holding yourself back through self-imposed limiting thoughts and have convinced yourself you are not responsible for these thoughts. What you fail to realize is you are the only soul in control of your thoughts, so how can you in all truthfulness question my love for you when you should be questioning your love for self? I love you greater than you are aware yet I will never override your free will to act in accordance to how you desire to create your life experiences. Blaming me for your choices only serves to keep you in the world of illusion does it not? Just because you attempt to convince yourself that you are not worthy does not mean that I find you not worthy my child.

Rather than accept responsibility for your own co-creative power, you would rather continue believing an illusion that we are separate. Therefore I must not find you worthy enough of having all you desire. My child it is time for you to see your world through the eyes of truth and know what you are responsible for when creating your life journey. No longer does it serve you to hide behind the walls of deceiving yourself and justifying it on the illusion I fail to find you worthy. For as a child of the Almighty are you not as worthy as God? Are not all my children equally worthy and entitled to their inheritance of all that is? Yet rather than seeing truth for what it is, you would rather convince yourself you can only have abundance of anything from the hands of another.

Stop deceiving yourself and take responsibility for your thoughts to justify to yourself how you can limit yourself in the co-creative process. For when you can stand in the mirror of life and see my eyes reflecting back at you then you will know that as I am one with you, I am one with all that is. Therefore you must also be one with all that is, which includes abundance of money, joy, love, and peace. The only thing keeping you from experiencing these are the limits you have placed within the walls of your own path. Do you see a long road ahead of you filled with wonder and miracles, or will you continue to place self-doubt and fear in the cells of your creation? The choice is up to you.

Now as you stand at the intersection of illusion and utopia, how do you want to create your life? If you choose to continue living in an illusion, you cannot go back to deceiving yourself of the fact you were not aware of the co-creative process. If you look at the long road ahead where utopia resides, are you willing to walk along this path using me as your guidance system? Will you keep your communication open and ask questions along the way? Are you willing to leave behind the baggage where you carried many years of illusion filled burdens so many people and experiences placed upon you during your journey here? For what you desire my child needs no baggage. As you place the burdens of your old baggage down, you will replace it with an empty bag that will allow you to place the tools necessary to help another release their self-imposed burdens.

You are relinquishing many years of old baggage and replacing them with one small one where you will store knowledge, wisdom, and grace to share with another how they too can create their own utopia. For in your journey you will replace the old with the new. On your road to creating a new home where your soul resides, you will rebuild the foundation to hold your new partnership with God. This foundation will be so strong that nothing can tear it down. I will uphold you in your quest to remind self of your own magnificence. Your foundation will be established in a faith so deep and a courage so resilient, you seek me only for knowledge and understanding.

The walls in which you rebuild your new house will be formed from a truth of being in the moment of creation every step of the way and being deliberate in what you bring into this house. The walls of truth shall separate the dreams in your house rather than hide them. Each room will represent a new vision of grandeur for you to nourish and cultivate all of the dreams your soul can envision. Your new understanding that as perfect spirits having an imperfect experience through the illusion of the physical life, you are not a product of your experiences. The walls in your house will only serve to focus one by one on each dream your soul desires to create and paint that dream so colorful you will know it from your blueprint.

As you create utopia you will fill your house with the healing energy of colors that reflect your creative spirit. Each room signifies a chapter of your life that brought you love and is filled with endless possibilities. Repaint each room to signify the expression of your life ambitions and your new dreams. Realize as you fill these rooms with warm and comfortable furnishings, they represent the comfort and ease of you being one in the presence of your dreams. Allowing yourself to send love and light into every corner of your newly designed house will bring in a light you have never before experienced.

My child, see every room of your house as a newly renovated project where you tear down the walls of illusion and dust off the remnants built from deceit and fear. No longer does it serve you to attempt to bring in new ideas of love and joy and fit them into your old house. Begin anew with the colors you love, the light you desire, and the dreams you are creating for yourself. Realize as you are rebuilding your new house which holds your soul and all of your dreams, you cannot bring in old fear or it will create rot in your new rooms. As you are aware of creating new love and visions, never allow old habits to occupy your utopia. Just as you chose to create a new home for your soul, you choose to rebuild it with all that you love and desire.

The same creative process you once used to create a house that fell apart from its old illusions, is the same creative process you use to rebuild it. This will withstand anything that would desire to tear it down. Do not bring in the old illusions into your new home, for your soul can no longer withstand living in deceit. There is absolutely no difference between the creative process of deciding you are going to work today from deciding you will follow your path and discover your purpose. All of your decisions are created through the intention of thought, emotions, and actions.

You have a choice every moment of your journey as to how you will create your life experiences. Although you cannot control the actions of another or the environment around you, everything you need to create your dreams lies within. Rather than focus your attention on the fear and chaos surrounding you in this illusion filled world, choose to remain steadfast in your creation of utopia. Your state of mind will be filled with peace and joy despite your surroundings. Is that not what being in a state of bliss represents to you? Now choose to create your life from love and take responsibility as a co-creator to write your story filled with pages of love and miracles. I love you.

Lesson Ten
THE DREAM WALK-THROUGH

"Lucky, miracle, special... all of these words represent each and every soul walking the earth. Yet what differentiates the miracle workers and the lucky few, is the realization that these souls have tapped into a Source so deep within themselves nobody can ever remove their truth. Look at your kingdom through the eyes of truth. You will discover your "luck" lies within your knowledge that Source energy is waiting to share love and discover the power of your very existence."

Excerpt from Through the Eyes of Truth:
A Conversation with God about My Life, Your Life, and Discovering Our Purpose

Have you ever allowed yourself to dream a vision so magnificent that once formed the world outside of you would consider it a miracle? My child you each have the capability to create a life where each of you are mastering your mind and bringing forth love and joy in all you do. Yet instead of choosing to create your life with such mastery, you choose to reset your thoughts every day to the same fears and limiting thoughts you created the day before. You do this repeatedly until one day you believe an illusion that you can no longer create anything else. Is this what you desired when you chose to experience yourself as co-creators with the Almighty?

Stop watching the merry-go-round the world around you has created and align yourself with your own greatness. When you cease from seeking guidance from a world around you, only then will you seek truth through prayer from the world within you. I have witnessed so many souls create more of the same and continue to spread fear rather than love. You choose to either become like-minded with these souls or find your own utopia within the walls of your own soul. Which do you choose to live your life by my child? The choice is always yours alone to make. Yet you turn off your own ability to think, and choose to mimic the choices of the souls in the world around you. It is no wonder so many of you are feeling lost and alone.

You have chosen to walk away from self, yet question how it is you are not living the life of your dreams. Creating your own utopia begins with self, and in order to discover what utopia represents to you does it not serve you to go within? If I asked you today to drop all of your illusions and leave them at the door or your old house built from limits and lack, would you be willing to do so? You pray for my guidance often yet when I respond to you and instruct your soul where to find love and peace, you fear the unknown and choose to turn your back on truth – your truth. What if I told you that everything you desire already exists? Would you believe me or would you ask the world around you for their opinion and approval?

Prayer is where the intersection of fear and love meet my child. So often you chose to walk from our conversation in prayer and seek validation from another soul. When you chose to do this what were you seeking? Was it the connection of soul love that you can only establish with me or the validation from another that the voice you heard echoing in the silence of your heart was in fact that of your Creator? This is why the relationship you have with me is the foundation for which to build your house of dreams. If your foundation waivers or needs the strength from something outside of itself, then it is not strong enough to withstand the outside elements.

A foundation must be strong enough to withstand the elements from the world outside of itself while supporting the walls of many rooms. These rooms all hold many hopes and dreams and represent the growth of your spirit. If your soul's house cannot be built upon a foundation of love, strength and unconditional support, then your house of dreams will crumble. Yet look at your life today and ask yourself if the rooms within your own soul have all nourished many dreams and continue to grow in the realization of more to come. If you have not the evidence of creating dreams that only you desire to experience self through, then you must go within and strengthen your foundation through love and prayer.

Building your dreams from the inside out is much like a carpenter building a house for which to stand through many generations and many changes in elements from the world outside of itself. The only way for your dreams to flourish is to be built on a foundation of love, support, and rooms that allow enough light in so you may never desire to hide them in the dark again. Does your soul's house offer this foundation for which to build your dreams my child? Take notice and seek first the relationship between you and Source, and there I will guide you and build your foundation so nothing will ever compromise your faith again.

Are you willing to do this my child? If I knocked on the front door of your soul in the still of a dark and quiet night, would you open your door to me? Would you allow me to enter into the house of your soul and ask that you leave everything behind except for a single bag? One which will carry the only tools you will ever need to create the life you were meant to live? All I ask is that you leave your baggage at the intersection where love and fear connect. The only bag you are to bring is empty and open to all possibilities to create a new temple where your soul will soar in its truth of perfection.

This means you must leave old patterns of thinking that no longer serve you and be open to new truth. You must leave old fears behind that were instilled within you from another, and trust my way is the truth and the light. Mostly, you must be willing to relinquish the illusion that you are not worthy, and choose to honor self throughout the course of creation. Are you willing to leave behind old beliefs that you attempted at all costs to believe so another would love and accept you as their own? For your bag must be emptied in order to be filled with abundance, love, and joy. There is no room for old illusions when creating your new utopia.

For dreams reside in your imagination and the power to create them lies within your own soul. No longer are you to seek your truth in an illusion filled world, but instead rely on my answers to your prayers. So if you are prepared, then pick up your one bag where you will be placing tools necessary to build paradise in your reality. These tools will be labeled truth, love, faith, courage, and prayer. You need not a large bag for which to carry these, as you will use them to share with others and remind them how they too have the power to create the life of their dreams by first seeking me in prayer. Are you willing to do this?

Now in order to create your dreams and turn them into reality, you must realize that all you desire already resides within the walls of your own soul. You have only to seek the connection of that which you desire to manifest and through your thoughts, emotions, and actions will you bring into light that which your soul seeks in love. This journey you embark upon requires no money, fame, or validation. As you seek me within your soul you will realize your birthright is abundance in all of these and anything else you desire to call forth in your experience.

You must first seek to align with that which calls you, by going within and walking through the individual rooms of your soul. As you walk through the house of your dreams where your soul resides, take notice of every detail in the rooms. The architecture of your dream house must be aligned within you to the point where you recognize and appreciate every attention to the detail of each room. What does it feel like when you enter into the first room of your new soul's home? What dream is just waiting to be realized? As you walk through this dream, be as detailed as possible in how your life will appear when you are living within the reality of this dream coming true. By practicing your dream walk through, you will feel the emotions of already experiencing this, continuing the thoughts of already seeing it in your life, and your actions will follow into connecting with it and aligning yourself to it.

Lesson Eleven
CREATE A NEW NORMAL

"Seek to break destructive patterns of thought, and you will break free from illusion and allow room in your soul to create love. If you continue in the same patterns of illusion, then you will continue to create more illusion. You have no idea the potential your soul has to create a magnificent reality that will bring you greater love and joy."

Excerpt from Through the Eyes of Truth: A Conversation with God about My Life, Your Life, and Discovering Our Purpose

Can you remember a time in your life my child, when you wished for something so much, the thought of having it overpowered your senses? This desire filled your thoughts and consumed your emotions to the point that it seemed already present in your reality. As your perspective changed from lack to the awareness of experiencing the love of that very thing you desired, your heart filled with joy. You transitioned from emotions of *not* having to having this in your life just by changing your thoughts and emotions. Before you realized it, the experience of already having this desire became your new normal.

If you would look at your illusion and allow yourself permission to step outside of your own self-imposed barriers when it came to creating your dreams you would see this the same way. What would happen if you changed your view of already having your desired dream in your life today? How would you act and what would you do differently throughout your day knowing this dream was already a reality? Suddenly your heart would experience joy and appreciation for the manifestation of your dream. You would be filled with overwhelming love for self and for our divine connection.

Can you feel how different your new normal would be? You would focus on the love that fills your heart and relish in the empowering emotions. You would realize you are a child of the Creator and there is nothing impossible...only truth and endless possibilities are in your reality. Now I would like for you to close your eyes and just feel the emotions of joy and gratitude pulsing through your heart, and let this feeling overtake your senses. With every breath your new emotions of joy envelop you like a warm blanket across your senses. This is now your new normal and your role is to create the emotions of this happiness throughout every moment of your day.

How? By changing your perspective from lack to already having the experience present in your reality. As you transition your thoughts and emotions from lack to having, you bring in the experience into your life. The truth of manifesting that very thing you desire suddenly becomes a reality through your awareness of having it. I have said there is nothing you desire that does not already exist within you. However you must align yourself to the frequency of that experience you desire to have. In order to do this, you must be aware of the presence of that energy already resonating within the walls of your soul. You must transition from fear into peace, and allow every cell in your body to connect with the creation of that very thing that already exists within you.

My child do you now see the act of creating is merely aligning yourself to the desired outcome you wish to experience? Since that which you love is seeking you, then your role in the co-creative process is to align with it and remain steadfast in receiving it until it becomes a part of the whole. You are simply transferring the energy of your wish into the physical reality through the role of the observer and creator. Your thoughts must be so tuned into your dream that your emotions already feel its presence within you. Once the feeling of joy and love fill your heart, then your actions will align to receiving your truth.

In this creative process you are becoming consumed with new emotions of love and satisfaction, so these experiences become your new norm. There is nothing mentioned about another soul having to gift this to you or granting you permission in order to have this. Understanding this on a soul level will empower you to realize why you need not seek your dreams outside of self through another's permission or approval. For you to replace the old with the new allows you the courage to step into a new level of receiving your dream and being an active participant in the creative process. For you cannot leach on to another's dream if that soul has created it only for themselves. Nor can another claim your dream because they desired it once they witnessed it manifested in the world outside of them.

Now you realize why it is necessary for you to first seek the kingdom of God within and all else will be given to you. In order for you to claim your own creations, you must be in the mind of seeking and thus receiving it. If you are not searching for that very goal which is searching to connect with you, then you risk continually looking away from it. Part of the co-creative process is to become aware of what it is you are trying to create and connect your mind, body, and soul to the existence of that dream. You all seem to think this is a more difficult process than it really is.

If you are born of God and I am the Creator of all things, would it not make sense to you that the creative process for you should be simple and filled with love? Why would creation be more difficult for you than it is for me my child? For I am experiencing life through you, so you too have the power to create the life of your dreams. The problem arises when your dreams turn into limits and fear. You create more of the same and then blame your self-imposed limits on one another or worse yet... you blame your limits on me. In order to know what you are creating, you must be in alignment at all times with that very experience you wish to create. If you are not, then you are creating nonetheless. You have already learned that if you are not creating from love then you are creating more fear.

Now is the time to own your truth and have the courage to create the life of your dreams. Ask yourself what it is you would create if you knew you were a child of God and creation was your birthright? It is my child, and the life of your dreams is only a realization away. Push yourself in one area of your life this very moment, and then allow that new level of creation to be your new normal. As you create one area then you will create one more, and the ripple effect will spread into every area of your life. You need not tackle everything in one moment, although you are able to do that, as the difference between illusion and reality is only a perception.

Because you have learned to adopt new patterns of thinking then you must replace the old patterns of thinking with new ones that serve your greater good. If it appears easier to do this one piece at a time, then do what works for the illusion you are detaching from. Whatever serves you the most, choose to do that and make it your reality today. My child, you have chosen to stretch the parameters of your fitness into running a half marathon and upon making the decision, you strengthened first your mind to set the goal and your heart to follow through. Only when you committed through your thoughts and emotions, did your action follow when you ran 13.1 miles almost completely unprepared.

You needed to trust your intuition of that small voice whispering in the corners of your mind that you could set a goal and follow through with it despite the obvious lack of training. Now you set the goal every day to run you allow this routine to become your new normal. As you strengthen your body, you align with a greater goal that has been awaiting you all along. Since you tested the waters and dissolved the illusion of fear and limits, you realize the creation of any goal is the same. If it is easier for you to break the self-imposed barriers one step at a time through running, then do what works for you. Soon you will realize the difference between running a half-marathon and achieving any goal is the same creative process.

You must first decide to be a deliberate co-creator in the role of your own life, ask me to provide you with the navigation and the communication during this journey, and follow through with your own free will. For I cannot desire for you to accomplish a goal of bringing more love into your life more than you desire to have it my child. You have been allowed free will and it is entirely up to you how you choose to create your thoughts, decide on the emotions you wish to experience, and follow through with the act of creation. My role is to love you unconditionally and to be one with you as your foundation of love and light.

Are you prepared to step out of your old path of discomfort and limits and walk the road where you alone pave a new journey? You have only one bag to carry so your load is light and you can now fill your heart with new experiences that align with bringing more love and joy into your life. Stand at the crossroad between illusion and utopia and trust that you can create the journey you desire by being the only footsteps to travel on that road into self-love. You have nothing to lose but the old fear and the old illusions that prevented you from seeing truth. I am here to hold you, guide you, and carry you when you become weary. Are you ready?

Lesson Twelve
FACING YOUR FEARS

"The truth is my child, what each of you fear is your own soul's perfection. You are taught an illusion since you were children that you are not worthy of everything you love and which brings you joy. Fear is a powerful tool of creation, for it creates an illusion within your soul. It will cripple your spirit from moving forward and recognizing and receiving all the love you deserve."

Excerpt from Through the Eyes of Truth:
A Conversation with God about My Life, Your Life, and Discovering Our Purpose

Do you realize why you have yet to be living in an eternal state of bliss my child? It is fear that keeps you trapped in the confines of your own doubt. You have the power to live your moments in your own utopia. Yet the fear in your heart overwhelms your senses to the point where all you focus your energy on is fear itself. Since you are a co-creator in your life and you are aware through thoughts, emotions, and actions you can create anything, then you are using the power of your thoughts and emotions to create more fear. When you snap out of the trance you have placed yourself into, then you will realize you can shift into a place of love instantly and create more love.

It is difficult to acknowledge but so many of you have become comfortable being in an emotional state of continual fear, that you would rather remain in that fear than change your thoughts. The moment you become aware of what you are thinking and choose not to shift your thoughts to a place of love is the moment you realize the choice is yours to make. Yet rather than own responsibility in your actions you would rather blame my lack of love for you as being the reason you do not get the life of your dreams. How can you be such magnificent creatures of truth and deceive yourselves for so long?

The reason you have yet to experience your deepest desires and greatest dreams my child is because you have grown more comfortable chasing them and then blaming God for not having them. It has somehow become easier for you to feel out of control over your own life than to steer your course in the direction you desire. What part of having your dream turn into a reality frightens you? When you sit down and close your eyes to the awareness of already being present in the space of your dream, what makes you uncomfortable? For if you cannot sit alone in a quiet room and envision that very wish you desire to experience already being present in your life, then does it not seem more uncomfortable to you having to spend hours focused on that very dream?

Yet rather than spending time attempting to be in your own truth, you convince yourself of an illusion that I chose not to grant you permission to have that very thing which brings you joy. Why would I deny you the experience of love when I am all there is, and all there is has been created from love? Why would I deny myself the chance to experience more of myself through love? You have spent so much time creating an illusion, you would rather be unhappy and living in fear than joyous living in love. Does it not cross your mind to even ask yourself why you choose not to think about the very thing you desire to create in your reality? If you perceive yourself as being without a certain experience and desire to create that experience, then your thoughts, emotions, and actions should be in the creation of it.

Yet fear is such an overwhelming emotion that it drives you to avoid even imagining what you desire and bringing it into your life. What is it about creating utopia that frightens you my child? Could it be that the road you will travel will be one where you carry not the burdens of untruths from another? Or is it the familiarity of feeling guilty for desiring something better than you have witnessed other souls create in their lives? For in order to be accepted by the masses, one must be of the masses and not do anything out of the ordinary to stand out. You risk being an outcast if you choose to walk your road alone, and you would rather be in a crowd feeling isolated and alone then to stand alone and feel connected to your Creator.

Giving up of the old beliefs that no longer serve your truth is the biggest obstacle you had in the creation of your dream. Now I ask you to step out of your comfort zone beginning today and do something every day that you would have once considered uncomfortable. By forcing yourself to step out of your fear you not only empower yourself, but open yourself to the possibility of seeing something before you that you had not noticed before. When you walk your life in the same patterns of repetition each and every day, you become oblivious to the possibilities of miracles around you. Not only do the repetition of patterns create the same sights and sounds, but the same feelings of fear and limits.

By forcing yourself out of your self-induced trance you are in essence opening your eyes to the world of what is, rather than to the same world you have been viewing most of your life. The reason you see not the desired outcome of your dream in your life this very moment is because you are not looking for it. You have created a pattern in your life that only serves fear, thus creating more fear. If all you desire to look for are fear based experiences then you cannot see the world of possibilities filled with love that are before you. It's as if you trained yourself to only recognize fear and illusion. Continue in this process and you will believe there is only fear to create.

By stepping out of your comfort zone and facing your fear, you see that the memory of an old event that created strong emotions of fear are being kept alive through your attention to it. Seeing something in your mind's eye that creates love and focusing only on the emotions of love will create gratitude. Your fear stems from feelings of not being accepted by the masses and not feeling worthy enough. Therefore you desire not to risk breaking your own heart through increased hope. By not granting yourself permission to hope and become joyous in anticipation of having your dream, you break your own heart every day. Then you become comfortable in the emotions of being heart broken and convince yourself that you are better off not getting your hopes up in the event that your Creator finds you not worthy enough. The truth is that you found yourself unworthy and chose to create those experiences that support your belief.

Empower yourself by releasing your fears and replacing them with love. Focus only on what your life will feel like and look like when you already have that goal you desire to create in your life. How will you feel when you see yourself in this place of love and bliss? How will you carry yourself throughout the day, what will you be doing, and most importantly how will you be of contribution to another to remind them of their own bliss? As you and I are one, you are also one with another and can remind them how they too can create the life of their dreams. For it is one step away from fear and one step towards love. No longer be content with allowing fear to become your norm, for by changing your perspective you will bring more love into your life.

In order to do this my child you must realize there is nothing to fear. For I bring you not to the gates of love and bliss only to keep you locked out and seeing it from the outside in. You hold the key because you created this place where you can enjoy being a co-creator in your life, and bringing new experiences that allow more love into your reality. Cease from standing at the gate of your dreams and asking me for permission to enter. As the co-creator you must realize it is only separate from you due to your perception of separateness. Change your perspective and you alter your experience. Reach out and touch the walls of truth and stand among the trees at the entrance of this bliss. Know that you are one with all that you see, and if you are standing as one then you must already have that which your heart desires.

Choose to remain steadfast and see your world of possibilities through the eyes of truth rather than through the eyes of fear. For if you remain of the world and continue to see only that which the world around you tells you is visible, you will continue creating more of the same. Honor me and create your life through my eyes and I will reveal to you a world unlike any other. A world where miracles happen in the blink of an eye. For too often you have stifled your deepest desires because the world outside of you had not yet created your vision. Instead of seeking the creation of that goal within, you chose to ignore it and only focus on that which has already been created. As co-creators in your life, do you think it be my will that you cease from being that which you are?

My child there is no greater deception you have chosen to believe than that which prevents you from experiencing your greatest truth. As a creator in your life your role is to use your intention combined with your love and create every moment of those experiences which bring you greater love and joy. Yet instead you choose to sit back and witness the world around you creating fear and believe the illusion it is only fear you can create. Rather than use the power you have been gifted through oneness with your Creator to design a life filled with endless possibilities, you would rather believe the only possibilities for creation are what you see before you.

If you desire to create a beautiful vision that brings you love and abundance of all that is, you must carefully select your thoughts to create this vision. These thoughts must create a picture so vivid that the details are as obvious to you through seeing it in your mind's eye as they would be if you were standing in front of it in the physical world. This picture must contain the details of every room in your house which you consider your physical world. Walk through each room and feel the emotions of already being in this place of solitude and joy. Take notice of the light shining into the corners of the walls and feel the warmth of the floor underneath your feet.

When you can walk through every room in your dream house and feel not the fear it represented to you once before, then you know you have connected with this on a soul level. Since you and I are one and I am one with all there is, realize there is no separation between you and this dream. Connecting to my love and experiencing the peace and joy of already being one with your dream will in fact connect you to this greater than anything else you can do. As you use your creative power through your thoughts that bring in the detailed vision of already having this, you are creating the connection between you and that which you desire. Replace the fear with love and you will experience only love for this new dream.

By allowing yourself to experience new emotions of love, you in turn open your heart to greater love. This love cannot be bought or earned my child. For you created your dream from the depths of your soul and have only to enter into your bliss to enjoy the essence of your truth. No longer desire to fear but instead become one with love and gratitude. Be ever grateful for your new experience of already having this dream even before you see it in the physical world. For my word is truth and will be honored through the journey of love. By thanking me for your blessings before you even touch them in the physical world, you align yourself with your highest truth of all that is.

You seek me with all of your heart and you have discovered me present in your reality. Hold on to the truth of my existence within you and you will soon see your world change according to your new beliefs. You desire to know what it is to create a miracle my child, but I tell you the moment you created the miracle is the moment when thought and love joined on its behalf. Now your actions must follow in the creative process which includes seeing only the presence of your dream before you and nothing else. Do not waiver and be ever mindful to remain aware. Soon the fog will lift and the veil of illusion will no longer separate you from your reality. Stay focused on seeing only that which brings you love and you will see only love in your presence.

This evidence of love will reflect back to you in the physical manifestation of that very thing your heart desires to experience. For you cannot seek truth and turn your back towards the evidence of that truth or you are deceiving yourself and will remain in denial until you change your mind and desire to seek truth once again. Your truth is that very thing you desire to see manifested in your reality is already very much present and seeking you as well. Keep your eyes and heart open for you know not the hour when you will hear the knock on your front door and stand in awe as your gift is being presented to you. The journey was complete the moment you prayed for this my child, now be alert and aware every moment. For the messenger will arrive when you least expect him bequeathing this gift to you.

Lesson Thirteen
THE ILLUSION OF TIME AND SEPARATION

"How can you worry yourself over a moment that does not even exist in its entirety? Time is an illusion. You create your future experiences within the moments that actually exist, rather than worrying about the time that has not yet been granted to you."

*Excerpt from **Through the Eyes of Truth:
A Conversation with God about My Life, Your Life, and Discovering Our Purpose***

What often separates you from your desired dream is not the fact that it has yet to be created, rather you have yet to connect yourself to what has already been created by you and for you. My child, you live in an illusion filled universe where you have convinced yourself of the falsehood, that if you do not see the dream in front of you then it has yet to exist. In fact the opposite is true. Your dream already exists and is very much alive, yet your role is to align yourself with that dream and already see it within your life. Then your perspective will shift from not having to already having that which you desire to create. Nothing separates you from your dreams greater than fear and the illusion of time.

I have already explained to you that time is an illusion and yet you build your entire physical existence on the illusion of time. You convince yourself that you do not have enough time to do those things which bring you great joy and love, yet you control how you spend the moments of your life. How can you tell yourself you have not the time to dedicate to creating your dream and then choose to dedicate that same time to creating fear? If you realized the amount of time you spend on memories that bring you fear from events already taken place, or even the fear of moments to come, you would see how you spend your time. The purpose of time is to allow you to measure your moments being co-creators in your life.

By choosing to live in the present moment and visualizing already having the dream you desire to experience in your life, you are making use of your time to be aligned with the creation of that dream. However if you choose to squander your moments by creating fear then blaming another for your lack of time, then you alone are responsible for the creation of that fear. By aligning yourself to the reality of that which you desire to experience has already been created by you and for you, then you spend your moments in the truth of living that creation. You need not see it immediately in your physical presence to know with all of your mind, body, and soul this vision of creation is already yours. You need only to remember that as one with your Creator, you can align with my presence and you will feel the creation of this dream turn into a reality.

Because you are so accustomed to being present in your physical world and basing it as reality, you sense the separation from your dream. Reminding yourself of the truth that you are already present in the love of this dream will shift your awareness from not having, to already experiencing the joy and love this dream brings into your life. Make this such a reality that you no longer feel comfortable living in an illusion of separateness. When you think about every detail of your dream, what do you see yourself connected to the most? If your love for water allows you to enjoy a dream home that only you can create, then create the detail of walking out of your back door into the beautiful pool. Feel the cool water as it touches your toes and tingles your spirit.

Take this vision further and feel the chill of the cool water covering your body as you step into the wonder of enveloping yourself in the comfort of it. Feel the gentle breeze from the ocean air brushing up against your delicate skin and hear the caressing sounds of a water fountain creating a melody to your ears. As you swim out into the center of the pool, feel the warmth of the sun on your skin and see the reflection of light shimmering across the pool as it glistens with every ripple of water you create. Can you smell the light ocean air as it crosses your senses and the brush of the tropical plants shuffling against one another in a dance from the gentle breeze? As you lay on your back and float, how does the water feel against your ears? Do you enjoy the freedom as you look above to the endless heavens overhead?

Take this one step further and feel your hands pressing against the water as you giggle in delight of this dream being yours from the creation of your heart and mind. As you observe the clouds overhead aligning to provide you protection from the sun, how does it feel? You have created a vision through your thoughts, emotions, and action of writing that will allow another to remember their own creative power? What does this pool represent to you as you bask in the glory of the water and appreciate life for the wondrous gift that it is? How can you come from a place of contribution as you relish in the truth of the fact you and I are one, and through perfection can create anything?

My child, as you relish in the feelings of wonder, empowerment, and gratitude do you desire to take a walk out onto the beautiful dock just several steps away? As you hear the sounds of water splashing against the pool as you make your way out towards the beautiful dock, what is it you see? More importantly, what do you feel? As you make your way slowly to the dock that houses the enjoyment of fun and thrills it will bring, what does your heart feel? For in this visualization you are not only connected to your passion but also to your purpose. With your purpose being to assist another soul in remembering their own perfection and the truth that they are not alone, you feel this stronger out on the dock.

As your words have sparked a ripple effect by reminding one another some of the most important truths you have forgotten. I hear and acknowledge all prayers. I love you beyond measure and seek not perfection from you but only seek to be in communion with you. I am all that exists and I experience life through each and every one of you. Since I am one with all there is, and I am one with you, then you are all connected as one. There is no separateness other than through your perception of being separated. Knowing this, you discover that the journey through life never ends, it just takes on a different form of energy. Nothing separates my love from you so nothing separates you from the love of another; not in life and not in the death of the physical body.

As you stand upon the dock of your dream and observe the vast body of water surrounding it, you feel even more connected to your purpose. For your journey through this dream was to be a powerful co-creator in your life and to remind another soul of their own truth. They are never alone and I hear their prayers and cherish any moment of connection they allow me to have with them. For your passion led you to your purpose to inspire souls into remembering their own truth. As you stand in awe and in complete gratitude for the manifestation of your dream, you watch the sun set on the horizon and know that my will be done through you my child.

For another soul who once stood upon these steps too had a vision so grand as to remind another of their own connection to the divine. Since you are all connected as one through me, this soul knew the individual roles you play in the creation of what some would consider to be a miracle. Just as a complete physical body has different legs, arms, and hands which serve a different purpose, they are still connected to one body. The legs allow movement towards another journey while the arms support the love for another while holding an embrace. In your case the hands allowed the complete story to be written word for word before this dream became a reality for you.

Now as you stand in awe on the dock of your dream you take notice of the setting sun and the dimming light. Although you may appear as a small piece of a large body of water you are a vital piece none the less. For each of you play a role in the creation of miracles and yet honor yourself not. If you could only see the vision I see through your lives, you would laugh more, love stronger, and dream bigger. For there is not a soul who has ever lived whose role was not vital in the creation of love. Every thought and emotion you send out creates a ripple effect far beyond what you can envision. If you realized the power of your actions combined with those thoughts and emotions, you would create your own visions which would stand among the stars.

These words needed to remind another along their journey through life that they are never alone. For even in your walk across the dock and the peace you are experiencing this very moment in the realization of your dream turned reality, you were not aware of the illusion of time. You created the connection of already having that which you desire to be manifested in your reality through your thoughts, emotions, and action of writing it out. It was only when I brought your attention back to your physical body where you realized you were in your office writing these words. Yet the illusion of separateness was gone and all you experienced in these moments was the reality of your dream.

This my child is how you allow yourself to connect to reality when existing in a world of illusion. When you can understand you are energy beings having a physical experience, then the physical no longer limits your experiences. You utilize the creative power of your mind, body, and soul to create the connection of that which you desire to see manifested in your life now. This is the true definition of utopia my child. Experiencing a state of bliss despite what the present situation in your life appears to be. For as everything is energy and created from energy, nothing remains the same unless you repeat patterns of thoughts, emotions, and actions to create sameness. When desiring a new experience and a new dream, you must change your patterns to reflect your awareness of already having that which you desire in your reality now.

Practice any dream you have and take the details step by step into the individual rooms of your soul. Create the connection from your thoughts and your emotions so you can create oneness with your dream instantly, despite what physical evidence may appear. By shifting your perspective from lack into already having that dream, you in essence create the connection and bring it to life. Create the patterns every day to support your grandest vision and rely less on the world around you and more on guidance from your Creator. Soon you will transition into your reality where your dreams surround your life and you experience an abundance of love and joy.

Lesson Fourteen
WHISPERS FROM HEAVEN

"Let every soul be reminded that although they may walk through their journey of life feeling lonely, they are never alone. Children are sending signs through teddy bears, boys are leaving baseball gloves in odd places, and parents are sending roses to their children. Animals that have crossed over are sending their favorite toys and even other animals that need rescuing in the physical realm. There are signs everywhere and these recipients of those signs are so immersed in their own pain that they often fail to recognize them. The teddy bears are being placed gently back on the bed from where they fell, the baseball gloves are being placed back on the shelves, and the smell of roses becomes just a figment of someone's imagination. The stray animals are being left on the streets and the dog toys are being given away without notice of why they were even discovered."

Excerpt from Heaven Scent:
Love Letters from Beyond

My child what is it you desire that you believe you have not already present in your reality? For part of understanding creation is knowing that which you wish to experience has already been created for you and by you. As you and I are one and experiencing your life as extensions of one another, would it not serve you to see your life through the eyes of truth? If you are aware of our union then how can you not be that which you desire to create? If you wish to know being anything in the physical world, realize it must have first been created in the spiritual realm with energy. Since you are born of energy and you and I reside as one, you must already have that which you desire. The only reason you see it not in your present reality is because you are not aligned to the energy of that which you seek.

Close your eyes and experience the feeling of already having that experience in your present moment. Relish in the emotions this evokes within you. Now as you feel these emotions, truly embrace them and breathe them in and out of your soul with every breath you take. This emotion of love now becomes connected to your breath and to your thoughts. As you align yourself with that which you cannot see, I would like for you to say a prayer of gratitude and be thankful for the experience of already having this. There is a difference in a prayer of request and a prayer of thanks. For one represents lack and the other represents already having that which you wish to experience.

In your case my child, you desire to experience creating something so grand both for you and for those who you desire to inspire. Yet I already connected you to these dreams many years ago. Knowing this, why is it you choose not to align yourself to them and be grateful in receiving them? In past it was fear that kept you from consciously connecting to that which you desired to possess. Now you realize the truth that you and I are one, just as I am one with every soul who has ever been. In order to understand the creative process you must know God, and to know God you must know yourself as one with me. This has been difficult for you, as most of your life was spent adopting the illusion that you are not worthy of having all that you desire.

You knew on a soul level this was in fact illusion but you found the emotions of fear so overwhelming, that you chose to relive the fear by repeating patterns of creation that would support you not being worthy. Now you look upon your life and stand in awe that you saw it not for the complete truth from the beginning. Knowing what you understand now allows you to empower another to change their perception, thus change their life experiences. Your story in the book of life was to write out your greatest dreams and create them thought by thought and word for word. Understanding everything you have been taught about God was in fact based on fear and fear alone. For how can I be all that I am and not have all that I have?

Yet as a child of God you chose not to see yourself through the same eyes of truth that I see you through. Have I not told you that you and I are one and as a child of all that is, abundance in all you seek is your birthright? You dared to embark on a spiritual journey that called on courage and walking your path alongside me. During your trip you discovered your own internal guidance system through my words, and now you have chosen to see your world through eyes of truth. Through the eyes of love. Realizing the complete picture of creation not only allows you to connect to truth once again, but to fully embrace communion with me in all aspects of your life. To know God is to walk with God as your guidance. To love God is to love self unconditionally. To honor God is to own your creative gifts and embrace your individuality.

For you need not another to grant you permission to create that which you alone have designed for yourself. You need only allow yourself the courtesy of understanding that in order to receive your blessings, you only have to say a prayer of thanks for already having these things. If you desire to experience your creative energy through writing a best-selling book, then say a prayer of thanks for already knowing your words are inspiring others. They are inspiring you. If you desire to own a new home on the waterfront of a beautiful river, then be in continual gratitude for that house and design your life as if you already have it in your possession. If you desire to be in a loving relationship with me so profound that you know not where I end and you begin, then be forever thankful for our communion.

Each soul has the ability to create an abundance of love and joy in your lives. Through free will you get to decide what emotions you desire to create. I will never seek to break my covenant with you, rather to love and guide you along your journey. Whatever you desire in love my child, you can create. Until now you have been creating from the overwhelming emotion of fear, so you had more experiences of fear in your life. Now as a soul joined in one heart with your Creator, your emotions of love and gratitude have tipped the scale of fear. Now love is the primary emotion creating your life.

When you cease from seeing me separate from you is the moment you will move mountains just with the faith of a tiny seed. No longer do you feel guilty for creating love, but instead you choose to assist others in creating love in their own lives. By following your passion of writing, you have been led to your purpose of reminding souls of the divine connection between them and their Creator. Through your love for truth have you been led to discover your journey in faith. You did not seek validation and courage from another, but recognized my voice calling to you in the still of your silence. Then you did something very few have had the courage to do. You listened. Only when you chose to silence your own voice and heed my call, did you become aware of the truth of your own existence.

Every soul needs to be reminded of their own perfection. Even if you reach one soul then that particular soul was the most important reason for this journey. Your faith allowed you to walk in truth and own that which I have created specifically for you. In the presence of love there you created more to love. Even though this journey appeared to have been walked alone, you saw not the souls who have supported you along the way. These are the same souls who know what it is to dismiss a dream and deny self until it was too late. Now these souls desire only to remind those they love that there is no separation. They are still united through me in the power of love.

For through your faith were you able to understand the union of love after your mother's journey on the physical plane had come to an end. As your purpose is to remind souls of the power of prayer and the oneness with their Creator, so your purpose is also to remind another they are never separated from the one they love. Union is the connection of oneness of all that is. If you believe the truth that each of you are united as one through the power of God, then you must realize you are united as one. Whether you are experiencing your journey through the physical life or on the energetic level, you are all connected to one another through me and I through you.

My child there is a current of fear spreading across your world like a wildfire. Too often souls will turn on the television to witness the destruction of human life crossing their screen, and their first emotion of the day becomes fear. As they progress throughout their work day, they speak of that fear and devastation so it creates more fear. Then they will meet their partners at the end of the day and continue to discuss more events of fear until they have created an entire day in fear. Before they go to sleep, they tuck their family into bed and turn on the television again to witness more of the same, until they cover themselves with a blanket of fear.

Continue creating these patterns of thoughts and behavior day after day, and you will understand why fear has become the major focus in your world today. What these souls fail to understand is the same power they have to create fear in their lives can also create an enormous amount of love. The scales have been tipped towards more fear and messengers are spreading turmoil like a wave of destruction. If you can each stop and take notice of how you are patterning your lives, you will notice the same energy you used to create the emotion of fear in your lives, you can use to create love. The words in this book serve not only to remind souls of their truth, but to create a ripple effect of love throughout the universe as you know it.

I have watched you cry in silence as you wonder how your lives came to be in such a place of sorrow. Yet you tune out my message when I speak truth into your hearts. You somehow dismiss my message as your own imagination creating a falsehood and refuse to admit that where I am, you are present as one with me. The tears you shed are the result of not trusting your own soul whispers. If you refuse to hear me then I cannot share my truth with you. In order to get your attention I needed to use the words of one soul who learned to trust in my voice and honor the passion and purpose to connect with me. These words have made way to your heart and now to your soul, as you understand they were written for you my child.

What if this creation of what the world would label as a miracle, was in fact my way of connecting with you once again and snapping you out of your fear based trance? Would you listen or would you tuck my whispers resonating within your spirit away as you have for so long? Until you can awaken your soul to the truth of life as you are living it, how can you alter your thoughts to create anything but more of the same? My child now is the time to open your mind, heart, and soul to the possibility of all I have been sharing with you as my words fell upon deaf ears.

You are one with your Creator and therefore one with every soul who has ever been. You are only experiencing self through the power of your own free will, in order to understand yourself as a perfect part of the greater whole. As you have grown accustomed to creating your life out of habit, so can you change your habit and create a new life. I have shown you evidence of this throughout many lifetimes yet you choose to believe an illusion that somehow you are not capable of doing the same as those who create love and abundance. How can I as your Creator choose to make a part of me complete, and another part of me without completeness? As a perfect spirit having an imperfect experience, you are not meant to be perfect in order to live a life of love.

You have only to choose your thoughts, emotions, and actions to support the love you desire to create and you shall experience this. In order for me to get your attention I had to use the words of another soul who was willing to document her journey so you may have clarity about yours. I needed to prove to you once and for all that there is nothing you can ever do to separate yourself from my love. You have only to call unto me and I will hear you. Yet if you choose not to be in union with me, then your free will allows you to create your life in the manner in which you choose. This is how one soul can create a dream the world would consider a miracle. By honoring the faith to do and seek the love for a greater vision only experienced in the mind… until now.

For you will read these words and a part of you will question whether or not they are written for you. My child, if I can create all there is as being one with all there is, can I not also create a moment in time when my love for you is reached through the purpose of another? This same soul lives in a world like you, where fear can be the overwhelming emotion. Yet chose to focus her thoughts on visualizing a beautiful dream where she could enjoy her greatest passions. Her emotions focused on experiencing love for the creation of this dream before it even became evident in the physical world. What will you do when you receive your call to change your world within, in order to change the world without?

Will you continue to reside in your house of fear or will you push beyond you own patterns of self-imposed limitations and realize I am within you? For I am love in every form. By connecting to love and all that love represents to you, more love will be created in your life through the power of your own hands. I send what you would consider to be miracle workers in front of you every day, yet you disregard them as being special or different from you. Yet have I not told you that as you and I are one, you are one with all souls connected through me? These messengers come to remind you of your greatest gift, which is the power to create as a child of God all that you desire.

Only now you realize what you desire has been fear and you can alter your course by changing your patterns of thinking, feeling, and acting. Whether these souls connect with you in dreams, on the television, or in your presence for a brief moment, they are serving their purpose to be in union with you. How can you witness the love of a man proposing marriage for the love of his life on the internet and become emotional, if it were not for the connection you have on a soul level? How can you see a child burst into tears when receiving a puppy they have desired for so long and not cry tears of joy with them as well? As you may never meet these souls on a physical level, you were connected on an emotional level to the point where you felt their joy. How can that be if you are completely separate from one another?

Whether you are on a physical journey of the soul or on a soul journey in the spirit world, you are all connected one to another.

There is nothing more a soul desires than to experience love. Once souls cross over through the veil of illusion into the light of God, there is only the experience of pure and undeniable love. These souls desire nothing more than to let those left behind know that they are at peace and in the warmth of the Almighty. If you choose to heed not my voice echoing in the silence of your soul, how then can you allow the love from another to connect with you and let you know they are in a place of eternal love? For as I connect with you on a soul level, so they do as well.

Lesson Fifteen

WHAT WILL YOU CONTRIBUTE?

"If you wish to experience more abundance, then share your abundance with others. Whether it is abundance of love, energy, faith, inspiration, or joy. Share it without ceasing. From those actions you will receive abundance many times over in ways you never even imagined."

Excerpt from Through the Eyes of Truth: A Conversation with God about My Life, Your Life, and Discovering Our Purpose

Can you imagine a life my child where all is a perfect state of being? There is no fear and the separation between illusion and reality is as evident as black and white. In this perfect place and state of mind, your soul dances to the truth of its own existence. Limiting thoughts do not exist and you are aware of being in unity and oneness with your Creator. In this beautiful and majestic state of being your presence is enough, and you replace the act of doing with just being. Can you envision such a euphoric place?

If you open your awareness to the truth of all there is, you realize a greater presence than just yourself. Through your awareness of possibilities you understand there is a grander purpose to your existence than being limited to what you perceive. Even though you see not the physical picture in your illusion of what I am sharing with you, the possibility of its existence becomes so real to you that your physical body reacts as if it were in front of your very eyes.

Yet how can your body react to something that your eyes fail to see in the physical form? Could it be that your soul remembers its own greatness through the truth that you are connected to the Source of all that is? Yet even though your eyes see it not at this present moment, the thought of being connected to something greater than yourself evokes a love and comfort so deep it stirs your soul. Even though you cannot see me through your physical eyes, your body reacts to a love so pure in the truth of knowing you and I are one. You may scan the room and look for evidence of me, yet you know deep within your heart I am one *within* you.

Is it possible that through glimpses of truth you are aware of the knowing there is nothing to be frightened of? Could it be said that somewhere deep within your soul, you know the unconditional love I have for you? Somewhere within the depth of my love you know you cannot do wrong. For you are not that which you do but are that which you are. You are perfection and the journey of the soul is to experience your own perfection. If you knew you could not fail through your life journey, how would you live your life? How would you create your grandest vision if you were aware of the truth of your own perfection? That as a child of God, abundance was your birthright and all you had to do was claim it first within the walls of your soul.

You would stretch beyond the limits of your teachings and reach for the wings of your own imagination. Rather than fear not belonging to the approval of the masses, you would relish standing on your own and paving your own path through the roads that only you can create. You alone would realize your own perfection. Rather than seeking to be validated from the world outside of you, the dreams you created would be guided through the reality of having me as your only co-creator. Think about your journey through life and what you would be capable of. Now make it your new reality.

Understanding the beauty of creation is more about the experience of creating love than it is about possessing something of value, what do you desire to give of yourself for the equal exchange of that value? For if you desire to know yourself in the truest sense of love, then your soul craves the knowing of creating love in exchange for love. Consider this an equal exchange of energy my child. As you cannot create fear from love energy, so you cannot create love from an energy of fear. Anything you wish to experience in the form of love must first be made manifest from love.

Yet so often a soul will look into the world outside of self, and seek to experience love from the creation of another's energy. These energy vampires believe it is their right to claim something of love created by another soul, and wonder why they receive it not. Furthermore, these same souls will dare create from an energy of lack which produces fear, and not receive that which they feel entitled to have from another. Rather than seeking to understand the truth of their own creation, they blame it on my will that they are not worthy of receiving what they desired. Not understanding they received exactly what they created, even though it may not have correlated with what they desired.

In order to know you are creating something you desire to experience from the energy of love, then you must be in the creative process and giving something of love from within you. For instance, if you desire to create your grandest vision as an artist and wish to enter an art competition, you must create your masterpiece from such a place of love that the outcome of your art will evoke a sense of love… from you. Once you experience the love in which you have created, it becomes not important as to whether or not you win the coveted prize from another. The soul's expression of creating from love was ultimately experienced by you, and it matters not that another failed to acknowledge it because you the creator felt the emotion you sent forth.

If you wish to apply for a job that you love and can envision yourself enjoying throughout the days of your life, then you must know what part of your love you are willing to give in order to create love for your own soul. Whether it be your love for your craft, your love for the company it represents, or your love for creating abundance using your talents, you must first be willing to create the experience of love in order to have that experience returned to you. So often you will ask God for a request you think you desire to experience and use the name of Jesus to support this request. When you receive it not, then you question whether or not your prayer was even heard. Then take it one step further and wonder why I thought you not worthy enough to grant you this request.

My child using the name of Jesus to claim something you fear brings it not to you because anything born of God represents love. If you have not created that which you seek to experience, you must first go within and create the experience from love and you will receive that which you have created in love. What often occurs is that a soul will witness the manifestation of something another has created and not understand how it cannot be theirs for the taking. Yet on a soul level, these individuals know the truth. That which they seek is not theirs because they ask in fear for that experience to be their own. If the experience is winning a contest that they feel not connected to, they will ask for their name to be drawn as the winner, yet all the while knowing they will not receive that which they have asked for.

You cannot lie to yourself. Yet many of you attempt to deceive yourselves daily and then blame it on the will of God that you did not receive that which you asked for. My child, my will for you is your will for you. If you desire to experience something in the external world then you must first create that experience from within. Not claim it once another has created the same experience you desire to have, as you cannot take that which is connected to another on a soul level unless they choose to gift it to you. Furthermore another soul cannot take that which is rightfully yours when you have created the experience from the love of your own creative power.

So much of the world today is filled with a sense of entitlement and not purpose. You seek the grandest expression of yourself outside of you rather than create it first from within. So now I ask you, what is it you seek to give of yourself in order to create love in its purest form? What gift from your soul are you willing to develop in order for another to know the love of God and love of self? For as you are all one and connected to one another through me, you inspire one another through first seeking love from within. Only when you have tapped into that love and harnessed your energy towards creating more to love can you and another feel the expression from that very thing you created.

For your goal is never self-serving when you desire to create an expression of self, birthed from love. Tap into your own soul blueprint and there you will uncover a treasure chest filled with gifts just waiting to be manifested. You need not seek it from another when your role in this journey through life is to become a creator to discover yourself. In order to know self you must create from self, using all that I have provided you from the treasure chest of your heart. Give unending from the love in your soul and you will not only create more to love, but will inspire another to recognize their own greatness from within their soul. Then you will know that very thing you have created on a soul level when it connects with you in the physical world.

If your gift to self and thus to the world is inspiration, then inspire another and another after them. If you desire to be loved, then share love so magnificently that you glow from the love from your own soul. If you wish to experience abundance in anything, you must first share that which you have. Then you will receive that which you have shared many times over. For your soul seeks not the possession of a material thing, rather the emotion of what experiencing that thing will bring to your soul. Ultimately if you are creating from a place of fear, that very thing you desire to have will bring you fear. How can it not when you called fear forth in your creative process?

In order to know what your soul desires, be diligent in coming from a place of love when creating any experience in your life. Always knowing that which you create and bring forth will first provide you the emotions you created it with. If you desire to win a contest, know what emotions having this contest in your life will bring you. Be very specific. If your soul wishes to experience empowerment, then share empowerment during the creative process. For you will empower not only yourself through the creation of this, but another will feel empowered by you as well. Then they too will seek to discover a creation within themselves that they can share in love with another. This is how the ripple effect of one person can make a difference and spread a blanket of hope and love in an otherwise fear filled world.

Lesson Sixteen
JOY IS NOT A DESTINATION

"They need not seek their love and joy from another. They have only to pray to Source and in the moment of silence, I will hear their prayer as I have heard yours. I will feel their prayer as I have felt yours, and I will answer their prayer through the form of love they desire to experience...as I have answered yours. Life is a never ending journey. The experience of knowing who you are is part of this journey of perfection. Ride the energy waves of truth to bring you to the highest waves of joy."

Excerpt from Through the Eyes of Truth: A Conversation with God about My Life, Your Life, and Discovering Our Purpose

How many souls do you know who create a sense of separateness from self when they are seeking to experience joy in their lives? The only reason you desire to experience anything my child is to know your soul on a greater level. This is why you desire to create any new experiences, to understand the power of creation and experience new ways of creating love or fear in your life. When you desire an outcome and bow your head to me in prayer of supplication, what is it you are ultimately after? For if you come to me seeking to know abundance by receiving more money, a better job, or the love of your life, you are ultimately seeking to experience joy through love in your life.

Far too often however, souls will distance themselves from the outcome they desire because they believe that joy is a destination. Joy is a state of being. Until you understand this, you will continue placing conditions on being joyous. For instance, so many of you say that you will be happy when you lose weight, you will be happy when you find the partner of your dreams, or you will be happy when you get a new home. Realize as joy is a state of being, you need not place the illusion of time into the creation of that joy you desire to experience. You can create it now at this very moment by placing your mind and heart into a state of being joyous.

Whatever the circumstance, you have the ability at any moment in your life to cease from creating fear and be in a state of utopia. Rather than convince yourself of an illusion that time is the factor preventing you from experiencing abundance of love and joy in your life, realize you can change your thoughts to create a different emotion. If there is something you desire to create in your life my child, such as a dream home in a beautiful waterfront location then claim your dream now. Own your paradise by experiencing already having this in your life and create the emotions now that you would have once you see it manifested in your reality.

When you awaken see your life so detailed in that new home and feel the abundance of love and joy now. See yourself standing in your beautiful bedroom and then taking every step in detail as you walk down the stairs to get your morning coffee. As you walk past each room of the house, see the view so detailed that it brings joy into your life *now*. Hear the sounds of the birds singing outside, and take note of the light shining into the room as you smell the aroma of freshly brewed coffee. Enjoy the feelings of empowerment and purpose as you realize your destination was always at your fingertips. Make every detail so vivid that it brings the reality into your experience now. Do this enough times throughout the day that it makes you joyous at any given moment.

Anything you desire to create is available to you now because you are energy. You have the ability to manifest so much beauty and love in your life. Whether you are creating deliberately or through repetitive patterns, you are creating either love or fear at any moment in your life. Knowing what it is you desire to create and being proactive about the process will allow you a life of greater abundance. Yet you place conditions on love, and because you only understand your own perspective then you believe I do as well. This is why you wonder how those labelled as bad people can have a good life with many material possessions, when you consider yourself to be more worthy and have not even though you are a kinder person.

The difference my child is due to your perception of creation. You believe creation must be earned through your good deeds, but creation is your birthright and a state of being. Choose to be in a place of love and you will create abundance of many things from love in your life. Create from fear, and you will create more situations to allow you to experience fear from unworthiness and lack. I place no conditions on love. For how can I when I am all that is and am unconditional love? I would have to place conditions upon myself. I am all that I am. Would it not make sense my child that you are also born from love, and need not place conditions upon which to bring love into your own life?

You have adopted an illusion that love is separate from you and therefore you seek it outside of yourself. You seek love through negative relationships, unsatisfying career paths, or unhappy homes. Yet all the while during your search for love you become more detached from it, because the Source of all love resides within you. As you seek to be loved from a world that has yet to learn to love itself, you find more loneliness and fear. So you adopt those emotions as your new reality and learn to design your life from those feelings. Soon you realize you are standing alone amidst a world of millions who pass you by every day and have only to look through you.

They cannot see you for what you are because you have yet to see yourself. You pass one another on the street and miss the everyday Angels and messengers I send you, because you are too busy looking at your telephone devises. How can you question your life being in the manner it is today and wonder why I provide you not with the validation you seek from a world outside of you? What if I spoke tenderly into your ear my child and you heard my words permeate throughout your entire universe. Would you believe it to be me? Or would you shrug it off as your imagination and forget about the message because you saw me not?

What would your response be if I told you that I whispered truth into your soul every moment of your existence? I speak to you in the perfection of your dreams where no perception of separation between you and I exist. My words echo throughout every corner of your soul and every cell in your body, yet you hear me not. How can you hear my words when you have convinced yourself of an illusion that I speak not to you nor find you worthy? My child, the truth will be told through the heavens and earth so all who desire to know my voice will finally seek it from within. There you will know my voice as your own and my will for you as your will for self.

The love and joy you seek through the creation of your soul need not be separated through the illusion of time, space, or other souls. For that which you have created and that which I have chosen for you are already done… they are complete. Your role as a co-creator in your journey through life is to realize nothing will separate you from those gifts I have created with you, except through your perception of separateness. The moment you place your joy on a future time is when you are convincing yourself of an illusion, that you will never claim that which you desire to experience in your life. For time does not exist. So telling yourself you will be joyous "later" or have the experience of love through something you desire at another time, only tells your *self* that you grant yourself not the permission to receive that which has already been created for you.

Time is not the culprit rather the excuse as to why you chose not to receive that which was created for you. Realize you have the power to create in an instant, so how can time be measured as a tool to separate yourself from God rather than a moment in which to connect and create love. Listen to how you speak of that dream you desire to see manifested. Take notice of the excuses you have created to believe an illusion that you are separate from that dream. Do you use time to keep yourself from claiming that which is rightfully yours?

In your particular dream my child you have only to claim that which you desire by speaking so clearly of its existence in your life, that the illusion of separateness is replaced with the reality of oneness. Take yourself on a detailed walkthrough of your dream house now my child. Feel the cold hardwood floors underneath your bare feet as you walk room by room across the house. You realize the large windows represent the light that your soul experiences now. For in your quest to create your grandest vision, you realized the darkness within your soul needed to be replaced with the light of truth. Of my truth.

Only when you began replacing the fears with love did you discover light that once dimmed your soul and all of your gifts waiting to be celebrated. For in one room of your soul laid a beautiful book of words that needed to be acknowledged in order to light your soul and illuminate your path. In another room of your beautiful soul hid an inspiring story of love and faith in the everlasting that would one day inspire another to believe in the power of love and eternal life. Yet in another room housed the promise of your Source energy not only hearing your prayers, but being able to speak truth into your soul at any moment of your existence. You had only to trust my voice.

For this beautiful house was literally your dream house in every detail of the word. You created this house through your purpose and your passion for the written word. Inspiring another soul who will create their own dream vision through intention and prayer was a part of your journey. When you realized my words were inspired from truth, you were able to see the entire picture instead of the story chapter by chapter. For if I had laid in front of you the largest vision of your dream at the moment you were connecting to self, it would have caused you great anxiety and fear. Because of this, I needed to walk you through each room of your soul in the chapters of your story, and allow you to understand from a soul level the wondrous process of creation.

As you followed your path alone you realized at no point were you ever lonely, but filled with greater love for your God and for yourself. As you and I are one, so I am one with every soul discovering their own truth. I will be the Source of truth and inspiration for them, as they connect with me once again and walk their path to the power of their dreams. You just need to believe in your dreams as much as I believe in you.

Lesson Seventeen
REFLECTIONS OF GRACE

"Look around you, and see your world created by dreamers who began without a dollar in their bank account, yet with more passion than money could ever buy. You recognize these souls, and also realize you too can become anything your heart desires. You need only the faith to discover Source within your own soul, to provide you with all that you need to manifest that miracle."

***Excerpt from Through the Eyes of Truth:
A Conversation with God about My Life, Your Life, and Discovering Our Purpose***

Are you becoming more aware through your awakening of the power you have to create my child? You receive your greatest dreams and consider them miracles not because you failed to believe in your dreams but you failed to believe in yourself. For your dreams are not separate from you, nor do they have the power to exist without your observation and interpretation of them. As nothing exists in your reality without first you being the creator and the observer. Knowing this, how have you justified that your dreams were taken by another due to someone or something keeping you from experiencing them? Yet so many magnificent souls choose to disempower themselves by blaming their lack of accomplishing goals on something outside of their control.

When you stop seeing yourself separate from me and from your dreams, you will be able to move mountains in an instant. Your soul cannot deceive itself and so often you have chosen to chase down the manifestation of another's dream because the vision of it connected you to a greater purpose. Yet because you failed to identify what that purpose was and remained steadfast in your own self-discovery, you allowed the connection to cease when another claimed their dream. When you witness the world outside of you create beauty and wonders in their lives, what you often fail to understand is the connection you feel to another's dreams reflects something special in your own.

Rather than judge another who has won a contest or who has created nicer homes or bigger cars than what you currently hold in your illusion, allow yourself permission to connect to the meaning behind their dreams. For there must be something within you that connects on a soul level to having a nicer home that you have yet to realize. Maybe a home similar to the one you desire represents a place of peace and inspiration. Instead of dismissing this emotional connection, allow yourself to connect not to their creations but what that creation means to you. If you wish to drive a beautiful new sports car that another has, allow yourself to go within and connect the soul inspiration you are experiencing to your own creative power.

You need not your neighbor's car, as you have the power to create a car of your own that represents to the utmost detail what you desire to have. For there must have been something calling to your soul that inspired an emotion of love that for a brief moment created joy. Keep the feeling of this joy and go within your own soul to connect to what the joy means to your spirit. You are not connecting your soul to a material possession of another, rather to the emotion of love this material possession represents to you. As you embrace the feeling of love, seek to create more of the same by painting your own picture to the detail of what your perfect dream car represents to you.

Take yourself through the same process of envisioning driving that beautiful new car and touching every detail of its fine leather underneath your fingertips. What does the engine sound like when you start the ignition? What do the new leather seats smell like as you inhale every detail of this vision and create the experience of having your perfect car now. Do you drive alone or are you enjoying winding roads and the breeze of the ocean air with your loved one in the passenger seat next to you? What does the heat of the sun feel like with the convertible top down as you exhale freedom along the scenic road?

I tell you this my child, once you continue detailing every part of your dream to the most minute specification and hold this vision every day, you will manifest that which you are creating. The goal is to allow yourself the inspiration to become that beacon which ignites more emotions of love and joy in your soul. Follow this path as you would a game of *connect the dots* because one emotion leads to a larger inspiration within you. This car represents freedom of expression for you and the safety to drive to new destinations you have only dreamt of. It never represents just a vehicle, as you are energy beings created by love and desiring to experience new experiences of love.

Yet what often happens is that you will experience a glimpse of joy when you witness a car driving past you that you desire to own. If you have convinced yourself throughout your life that you are unworthy then you will never allow yourself to achieve having it. When you see it not in the presence of your physical journey, you assume the answer to your prayers was "no" and that I must not find you worthy enough to have such nice things. What you don't understand at that particular moment is that I placed that car in your presence to remind you of your worthiness. The belief must begin within you in order to connect to that car which has already been created for you.

Somewhere along your journey you became accustomed to no longer believing you could own an expensive and detailed sports car so you began taking notice of vehicles that you would then "settle" for. You observed only these cars for so long that you convinced yourself it was the only possibility and all that was available for you in this illusion filled journey. I then sent you a beautiful new car to catch your attention and to remind you of your magnificent ability to create the same type of car if not a better one for you. Rather than seeing this as a way to empower you by replacing your own self-limiting thoughts with truth, you began to convince yourself of a lie. You then believed I sent you this car to negate your worth. How can you be born of such greatness and live in a self-destructive illusion?

My child, you have prayed for such grace and love in your life, yet if you choose to only see fear then how can I provide you all that brings you love? If you cannot alter your perspective and realize you are the only soul who can empower or disempower yourself, then I will continue to show you love. Until you see yourself through the eyes of truth and know you are worthy of all you desire, then you will choose to only see that which supports fear. I will continue sending you messengers of truth until you finally recognize your own worth. You get to control your journey through what you choose to seek and how you choose to have a relationship with Source.

Yet you are so consumed by what you witness on the television and media, you have almost become hypnotized by fear. Your mind is used to seeing pictures of violence on television. You are teaching your children to become accustomed to this fear by providing them violence through games, thus putting them into an early trance of creating and accepting fear. Do you not realize that each generation will continue to perpetuate more fear until at any point you choose to create your life from love? The beauty and perfection of each soul walking this journey through the physical, is that you each know truth and need not seek it from one another. Prayer is the conduit for change and although you may inadvertently teach acceptance of fear to one another, you also remind them of their truth through the power of prayer.

I now answer your prayers in a way that will ignite more love into your awareness, and remind you that all prayers are heard and all cries acknowledged. Somewhere in your fear, you have forgotten that you too can create a blanket of love over this fear based illusion you have immersed yourself with. Now I send you a miracle that may appear to have been connected to one soul in your journey, but you will discover truth of your own perfection in this perceived miracle. Do you not think I hear every cry uttered through your soul into mine? As you and I are one, you have forgotten to hear my voice and have conversation with me.

What perceived miracle will capture your attention even for a brief moment to shake you out of your illusion? If I could show you how one miracle came to be, would you not be interested in discovering your own greatness? Furthermore, what if I covered your soul with the hope that you are as deserving to create love in your life as anyone you have witnessed doing the same? Would you listen, or would you continue to disregard these perceived miracles as random acts of kindness I perform for souls who you continue to regard as favored? My child I am going to shake you out of your self-imposed limits by walking you through a journey that only you can take.

Although the steps in this journey may be perceived to be of another's, you will know that I am reaching you through the depths of your own sorrow in order to remind you of your own greatness. When you realize this journey of another was meant to reveal the truth of my existence in your life, only then will you bow down to me in silence and ask that I reveal truth to you... your truth. For no other can provide you with the guidance to become your greatest creator than the Creator of all that is. You will witness the manifestation of another's dream and your soul will dance with the hope that you too can create wonders in your life.

Yet what you will soon realize is the journey of this soul who captured the attention of many was meant to remind you of your own greatness. Although you may desire to be chosen as this soul was for a specific path, I will also lead you to your chosen path that only you created for the expression of your soul love. You will witness an illusion based blanket being lifted to reveal the truth of all souls. Reminding you that every miracle resides within you and you are just as loved and honored as those you witness manifesting dreams in their reality. The only difference is they chose to listen to my voice echoing in the silence of their souls, and honored their purpose by following their passion.

Instead of being envious that you have not that which they have achieved, allow yourself to recognize the light of truth being ignited within your own soul. Know that all you need to do is go within and seek Source in prayer. Then you will follow your own passion to create a chosen path that you have yet to see, but know in your heart to be real. Are you ready to walk your journey into truth and love? You are a miracle worker and have awakened out of your illusion filled trance to recognize my voice echoing in the silence of your soul. Let us walk together my child and create the life of your dreams. I love you.

Lesson Eighteen
DISCOVERING YOUR TRUTH

"Look around you, and see your world created by dreamers who began without a dollar in their bank account, yet with more passion than money could ever buy. You recognize these souls, and also realize you too can become anything your heart desires. You need only the faith to discover Source within your own soul, to provide you with all that you need to manifest that miracle."

Excerpt from Through the Eyes of Truth:
A Conversation with God about My Life, Your Life, and Discovering Our Purpose

Are you now remembering the process of connecting the dots of your own soul blueprint to follow your path to the life of your dreams? Are you prepared to see life and the creation of dreams through the eyes of truth rather than through the illusion of fear? Take yourself on a journey within my child, where unlimited love and abundance of anything you desire resides. You need not see this journey yet in the physical world outside of you to know from every beat of your heart that it exists. Can you begin tapping into the emotions of love and joy this soul connection already has within you? If I pulled you out of self-imposed thoughts that created limits, how would you consider I do this in the kindest and most gentle way possible?

What if I showed you an example of something you could create that reflects the grandest vision for your soul journey today? This example could be something like a house you would connect to on a soul level, but could witness the creation of that dream from the ground up. Let us imagine that within the walls of this newly formed house lies the blueprint of a dream from one who created it on the physical level and one who created it on a spiritual level. Would you be interested in witnessing the birth of this design?

Better yet let us allow the design of this dream to represent a state of bliss. This dream journey will be created so you can allow yourself to witness the possibility of what you would have once considered a miracle. Now you will see the word miracle is as common as referring to every soul who chooses to dance to the song of their own soul calling. Let us take a beautiful house whose structure has lost its strength but the foundation is still strong. For this house is much like the body of every beautiful soul that has walked through the illusion of limits and lack of self-worth. We will witness the removal of the old walls and doors that once housed limits and lack and replace them with grand windows and light that illuminate a new way of thinking.

This dream would be designed as detailed as the building of a house where each room eyes of this house, and no longer will the rooms be kept hidden from the well of life. Look at these windows as your eyes and the removal of the walls as the removal of self-imposed limiting thoughts that have kept your dreams hidden in the darkness for so long. As the old walls and lumber of the structure are replaced with new strong beams of support, you see this as your new way of thinking and feeling. You are replacing your old patterns of negating me and negating yourself, with the truth of your thoughts now being open to my voice echoing in the silence of your soul.

Let us pretend that in your illusion you get to witness the rebirth of this house room by room so it now reflects a new way of thinking and acting. Instead of being limited by weak walls, your new house holds the strength of dreams. Instead of dimly lit rooms, the new windows in every room open up the possibility of new patterns of thinking and opportunities awaiting your soul journey. After the house is carefully redesigned one step at a time, it now stands upon a new journey and a new purpose than the one it had before. For this structure is open to truth and light, and its strength is greater than it was before.

From the view of this house, you can see a scene of majestic possibilities and endless ways of expressing love from your soul. Every room in this house now embraces the love you have for self and the love you have for the creation of your soul gifts. Yet if you look at this house and just see it from the physical world, it appears to be a structure much like any other. So in order to capture more of your attention and pull you out of your fear based trance, I will provide you an opportunity to own this house. You will glow from the excitement of knowing somewhere in your soul, you have ignited a beacon of hope that has filled your heart with joy. You no longer repeat the patterns of your old way of seeing the world through the eyes of fear, but allow yourself to focus on the chance of connecting to love on a greater level.

So every day you begin creating new patterns of thinking as you view this house, and dream of walking through the front door of this home and calling it your own. Somewhere in the depths of your soul you have found a glimmer of inspiration which allows you to smile with the possibility of owning that dream. Yet as you have discovered, you are not necessarily connecting with the structure as much as you are to your own truth on a soul level. Just as I provided the example of the sports car igniting a spark of hope within you, this house represents the same. Although it is one house being revealed to you just as the sports car was, it represents the truth of what you have hidden from yourself.

This truth being the miracle worker each of you are and the power you possess to create abundance of light, love, and inspiration in your own life. As the possibility of owning this house becomes real, you do something you have failed to do for so long. You pray. You reach out to me on a soul level and ask that my will be done to provide you this particular house in which to live. Yet due to your limiting thoughts you are still convinced that by owning this house, you will finally be worthy of love in my eyes and in the eyes of the world around you. As you pray daily for the chance to own a piece of luxury, your heart ignites with the passion and purpose of what your life would look like if you lived in this beautiful home.

This is where you connect with your truth and your current fear as well. As you envision yourself walking into each room of this lovely home you see yourself having family and friends who desire to be connected to you. Not only do you believe they see you differently, but most importantly you view yourself differently. You now see yourself as validated and worthy of having all you desire. Furthermore you see yourself being loved and validated by your own God. For if you have been justified by Source in receiving a material possession then you also must be worthy of having so much more. Now take a step back and see yourself standing in this house and connect yourself with the emotions you are experiencing this moment.

What does your heart feel like? Is your chest tight and constricted from anxiety or do you feel relaxed and loved? If you feel connected to Source on a deeper level, then you have created what this house represents to you now. You have connected to your bliss and your perfect state of being in love.

However if you feel anxious, then you have also connected to your fear and it has been revealed to you. Separate yourself from the vision of this house and connect only to that which you feel. This overwhelming emotion is the truth of where your illusion has brought you. If you are standing in your emotional sanctuary feeling bliss and love, then this house represents to you a soul connection with your higher self and with God.

However if this house represents fear and unworthiness then you have discovered the result of your patterns of thought, emotion, and action. What you have failed to realize my child, is the emotion you are experiencing at the point of creation is what you will continue to create. So if you are experiencing fear and anxiety, then you are in essence asking for more of the same by asking for this house to be yours. Like energy attracts like energy, and unless you alter your thoughts then you will continue to create more fear. So in essence my child when you desire to experience anything in your experience you must connect with the emotions of that which it evokes within you.

Viewing the manifestation of this beautiful new house allows you to see the world of possibilities through the eyes of a group of dreamers who have created this experience from love. These souls gathered on a deeper level to combine their purpose and passion. The current structure was built from an old pattern of thought, but now new thoughts have redesigned it to reflect a brand new house. These souls gathered to reflect back to you the possibility you have as a child of God to create anything your heart desires from the mind, body, and soul. They opened your awareness of seeing something you forgot you too could create.

Now this house does not represent your worthiness in my eyes child, but your perceived worthiness in your own eyes. For this house reflects back to you that which you see in yourself. If you perceive yourself as not being loved enough, worthy enough, or lucky enough to have something so special, that is what you will feel. However if this house represents to you on a soul level the possibilities of creating your own dream from the ground up, then you have empowered yourself through witnessing another's truth. The soul who will ultimately receive this house has already envisioned it and created it long before you witnessed the outcome of its existence. This soul connected to love on a deeper level. Through that love for self, for Source, and for you was this house built.

Have I not told you that you are all connected as one through the power of God? If one chooses to create a dream that not only honors the truth of prayer and the power of love, is it not worthy enough to connect to self and honor that which you love? For I cannot and will not give another soul something that one has created for themselves. Why would I? Yet once you failed to receive this gift you then blame your Creator that I found you not worthy enough in my eyes to receive something so valuable. My child, it was you who failed to identify your own worth in my eyes thus creating more experiences that allow you to feel unworthy. Rather than continuing to see your life through the eyes of fear, take notice and realize your destiny is being created by the very thoughts and emotions you are experiencing now. If you choose to connect with Source on a level of co-creation, then I will guide you to deeper waters and greener pastures than you can envision.

The journey to your grander self lies in the courage to walk your path with God and to seek guidance about your truth from within. Are you willing to do this? Now that I have captured your attention, are you willing to take the leap of faith and pray to me child to reveal your truth? Every soul is on a journey into remembering who you are and what you are capable of. You are not defined by what you have rather by who you are. As a child of God you are all perfection. What better way to reveal you own perfection than through the creation of a house of dreams? For your physical journey represents your house. The dreams you have hidden within the confines of your soul are just waiting to be revealed and brought to life. How? By your awareness of them and your connection to love on a soul level.

My child the story of the dream house lies not in the abundance of a material possession, rather in the creation of love. For this house represents a story of love, faith, and life eternal. For some will look upon this house as a means to an end, where they can have abundance of validation and material possession in which to make their lives easier. Others will view this as an opportunity to reconnect with Source and have a greater understanding of the power they have to create anything they desire through passion and purpose. Finally, some will look upon this place of utopia and see it as a connection to those they have loved and lost. They will look upon this story and realize it supports the love of those who have crossed through the veil of light and the possibility that although they are no longer connected in the physical, they are eternally connected through the great I am.

Whatever you see through this journey, realize that I make many attempts throughout your life to remind you that you are not alone. My child have I not reached out to you on a soul level to ignite even a possibility that you and I are one? There is nothing you can ever say or do to remove my love from you. For you are a child of perfection having an imperfect physical journey, to remind yourself of what you are capable of through the power of creation. In those moments you have cried out to me, I have not only heard you but held you tighter in my arms. Your soul has experienced moments of anguish as well as glimpses of love and light. You yearn to connect to your Source yet are in such a state of fear that I needed to remind you that I am one with you.

Find your truth, create from the power of your own hands, and honor your purpose of living your greatest life in the light of God. You are all one, and through me are experiencing a part of the greater whole. There is no separateness except through your perception of being separate. Use the gifts in your soul to ignite your light and inspire souls in the world around you. Come out of underneath the blanket of fear. Celebrate your life as you desire it to be. I am one with you now and forever.

Lesson Nineteen
CONNECTING THROUGH THE VEIL

"For so many souls who cross over the veil of light yearn to let their loved ones know they are loved and joyous. They long to reach out to you just for a token word to let you know they love you and are not gone but have only transitioned. These souls reach out daily to you through their energy, through whispering "I love you" into your ear, or through their touch that stops you in your tracks to take notice. Yet rather than acknowledge and trust your own intuition, you seek to have your connection validated by another. If someone else negates or even disputes your intuition, then you disregard the experience all together."

Excerpt from Living, Dying, and the Seasons of Change

As every beautiful song has a composer, still it cannot be sung without the willing souls who complete the melody. The composer is the author of the story of all life. This beautiful melody was created to remind each and every soul that you each play a vital part in the song of life. I cannot experience myself as that which I am without knowing every beautiful soul that is a part of my whole. You too have been a part of creating a melody comprised of many beautiful instruments. Some of you served to lend your beautiful voices to this song, while others designed the harmony, and still others the lyrics. There is not one soul whose role is more important than the other when it comes to creating a love language that will connect to every soul in sharing this story.

My child no longer buy into the illusion that your role is any less important than the soul who sings the song with one voice. For as you are all part of the greater whole, your journey never ends with the physical body. You are magnificent spirits having a physical experience that is to be cherished during the short amount of time you are in this present form. The act of creation is about abundance of love and joy. Even though you may play the role of a melody finding your voice, your soul sings loudly across the heavens and earth. No longer perceive yourself of being any less important on this journey through co-creation, than the soul who wins millions of dollars in a lottery or drives the car of your dreams.

You each play a role in reminding one another through inspiration that you have the power to create from thought, emotions, and actions all that you desire to experience. For so many souls leave the physical journey of life desiring one last call from the other side of truth. To share in the glory of all that is and to just shed light on the truth. You are all magnificent spirits and are all called to glorify God through living your life as you desire. However realize there is more to life than fear my child. Oftentimes there are glimpses of those who have crossed over to remind you there is no such thing as good-bye. You catch these glimpses of loved ones in your dreams, on a crowded subway, or whispering "I love you" into your ears. These moments of energy connecting to you are reminders that you are never alone. There is nothing to be feared.

Ask yourself of the possibility that if I reside within you as one and am one with every soul on this journey, would it not be truth that you are all one with another? Further if you pray to me and cannot see me but feel me as truth within your soul, there lies the possibility that those you have loved and lost also reside as energy within your environment as well? Even though you cannot see them, these souls who have loved you and still love you want only to remind you that you are loved. So often once they cross over the veil of illusion into the light of God, they desire to connect with you so you may be at peace. There is nothing to fear and all to glorify through the power of your own hands.

Yet even though these souls have already transitioned to the other side they are still a magical part of the symphony of life. For a song has many elements that combined together will orchestrate the most beautiful sounds the energy of life can create. Knowing this, would it not then be possible that although you see not these souls in the physical form, they are very much a part of this beautiful journey? Reminding their loved ones that life does not end with the physical body, nor do dreams end except by the creator of that dream. Follow the song in your heart and know that another has placed the melody there to remind you of your own greatness. If a beautiful melody is playing in the corner of your soul and you hear it not, how will you know the sounds of beauty you can express through the power of creation?

Every journey that leads you to know God and to know self is orchestrated by more than one instrument my child. The journey of your soul is to discover the melody playing within your heart and realize you too are a part of the unity of the music. Even though you witness another soul's creation of what you would consider a miracle, judge not the process. Most importantly cease from comparing the illusion of another to the reality of self. For you know not the truth of that soul and what passion they followed in their own heart to create a part of the beautiful melody. Realize you too play an important role in the music of life, and these whispers from the other side only serve to remind you that your role is as perfect as any other's. You have only to honor it and use your passion as your instrument.

You all have the ability to create a life of love and passion whether you are on the physical or the spiritual realm. Realize that creating love in a world where fear is the greatest ripple effect is your choice. The music you create in the orchestra of life will send light into the soul of another who will recognize something special within themselves and know their role is to connect with Source through prayer. By discovering that which you seek is already within you, the power is unleashed to create what your soul desires to experience. You are not limited to lack but can create anything your soul desires in abundance of love and joy. Use the instruments another has revealed to you not to compare yourself nor find yourself unworthy, but rather to remind you of your own worth. You will never compare to the world outside of you when it is all an illusion so do not judge yourself.

Instead, realize you placed these souls in front of you to remind yourself that you too have the power through the light of God to create all you desire in love. Honor the whispers of those who have traveled before you, and know they send you greater love than you can imagine. Remember my child, you are not alone. You are never alone so choose not to isolate yourself from your greatest Source of love ... your God. If together you can create a life of love through experiencing your greater self in this world of illusion, then you are in fact allowing your love to spread across the universe like a tide across the ocean. If you can envision yourself as a greater part of the whole you begin to realize how one act can create a ripple effect across the world. Choose to live in your own bliss and create love through acts of love.

Imagine knowing what you now understand at your age, and being able to impart wisdom to yourself when you were at the age of experiencing one of your greatest fears. What would you tell yourself to assist you in shifting your attention to that which frightened you to something that would soon empower you? Although at a young age you saw not the actual experience that would one day occur and bring you much joy, you would tell yourself to have faith, know you are loved, and to seek God in prayer so you need not walk this journey alone. Now ask yourself if you cross over the veil of illusion, which every soul will one day do, what advice would you gift to one you love to help them through their experience of fear and isolation? Would you not share the same gifts of love and light? Sharing knowledge through offering hope that they too need to have faith, know they are loved, and seek God in prayer so they need not walk this journey alone. If you would love yourself enough to go back in time and offer hope to self during your darkest moments, do you not think that I would do the same for you by allowing messengers of hope to bring you peace?

For you are all my precious children and I seek not to isolate you in fear but to reconnect you to the truth of your own existence. I am one with you experiencing life through your journey. Because you and I are one, you are connected to one another. Nothing separates you from the love of another through this journey except for the perception of separateness. When you seek comfort through connection with your Creator, I will send you more emotions of love than you could imagine. My whispers through your soul echo truth to provide you peace in this journey of illusion. Those you have loved and lost also seek to provide you comfort and bring you peace. They seek to offer love through a beautiful dream visit, a gentle and unexpected touch, or a whisper into your ear during a moment of emotional pain so great that you feel as if your heart has shattered into a billion pieces.

What better way to share in the glory of life and love, than to offer words of encouragement through a voice of someone who knows the depth of pain from losing their loved one. My child there are no coincidences in your experience. Acknowledging soul signs allow you to recognize truth. Despite any perceived experience of fear, there is something far greater to be experienced through love. For this journey through life is such a precious and yet magnificent gift. Yet how many of you see your life as this gift? Every soul who has incarnated in the physical experience will cross over to live once again in the reality of all there is. Realizing that death is not for the sinful, the negligent or the victims, know you too will cross over to be as one with me once again.

With that said, ask yourself how you wish to experience your life now? If you knew there was no tomorrow then what dream would you gift to yourself? Do you not think for a moment that so many souls who have crossed over the veil of light had dreams yet to be fulfilled? Yet from fear many realized their journey was to understand who they were *not* in order to know who they are. In other words, they experienced a journey through life with fear in order to know love as themselves. They only wish to remind you that this journey is but a veil of illusion, and you can create your life in the manner which you desire at any moment.

Honor your journey, love greater than you have ever loved, and dream grander than you have ever allowed yourself to dream. When your moment has come to cross over into the light of love, you will know what it was to live a life of exquisite creation. Cease from worrying about moments that are yet to come or worse, moments that no longer exist. Embrace every moment of this precious journey and honor yourself through celebrating your passion, your gifts, and your purpose to create love in abundance. Then your life will be filled with passion, purpose, and abundance. I love you.

Lesson Twenty
BEING IN ALIGNMENT

"Establishing your connection through the power of prayer and learning to decipher the whispers of my words into your precious soul, is the greatest peace you can bring to yourself. It allows you to extend your love to me and accept my love to you through the journey of this life. By establishing your connection to self and learning to trust in your soul whispers, you allow yourself to be connected to a greater reality. From that reality is where miracles are manifested and dreams come true."

Excerpt from Living, Dying, and the Seasons of Change

Today is an instrumental day for you my child. As you are becoming more aware of your own presence in the manifesting process, you perceive illusions that are present in your life. Rather than denying them, you are seeing truth as truth which allows you to change your thoughts. Once you identify an illusion through your thought process that has prevented you from connecting to all that is, you empower yourself. Have I not stated to you that you are perfect in who you are? Your perceived imperfections connect with what you do not who you are. For you are all a perfect child of God and have nothing to prove to another regarding your own perfection. Why then do so many of my precious children spend countless hours and abundant energy on attempting to prove to the world around them they are worthy?

You do this on your social media outlets where you post many photographs of yourself in order to obtain a response to an illusion? Once you post a photograph of yourself and the world validates it not, your immediate response is hurt due to the lack of support. If you do not receive as much positive feedback as you initially desired, then you react by either taking it down or sharing something else about your life that may get the feedback you desire. You spend so much time attempting to prove to the world outside of yourself that you are beautiful, successful, and worthy when you should be spending that energy looking within. Do you not realize the emotions you experience are your own?

If you fail to receive validation from another and your response is to feel hurt from that lack of support, do you not see it is you who lacks support towards self? The emotions you experience from the world outside of you is a direct reflection of your feelings towards self. When you realize this, you will use the reflection of the world outside of you as a guide to understand how you feel about yourself. Knowing at all times what you experience as a response to a powerful emotion such as fear, will enable you to seek truth within yourself and connect with me in prayer. For I find you a perfect child and an extension of me. How can you not see yourself through the same eyes of truth?

So many of you awaken in the morning to a brand new day not realizing you can create anything you desire. Instead of spending your first waking moments in prayer and being in gratitude for another opportunity in which to create your dreams, you thoughtlessly revert back to the same patterns you have used to create your life for so long. Choose to repeat your same patterns of thinking, feeling, and acting and you will create the same experiences. Be deliberate in your creation to the point where you are not only changing the way you think before your day begins, but plan your day exactly how you desire to experience it. Before you retire and go to sleep at night, plan your next day and how you will awaken in gratitude to a new opportunity.

You have every moment to choose to experience love or fear, and I witness you creating more and more of the same. You then become angry at your God for not hearing your prayers thinking my answer was "no." In fact the reason you continue creating your old patterns and having the same experiences are because you fail to take responsibility in your role of co-creation. Do you not think I desire for you to have all that your heart seeks in love? I am experiencing a part of my existence through every soul walking this journey through the physical illusion. I desire nothing more than to have what you desire. However I granted you free will in order to create your life as a perfect child, thus I will never prevent you from acting in accordance to how *you* desire to create it.

The moment you take responsibility for your own achievement is the moment you connect with the greater part of your ability to be a powerful creator in your life. For it takes the same amount of energy to create the fear you have been experiencing as it does to create love. Yet you are not comfortable creating love in your life so you choose to experience more of the same fear by repeating your patterns. This is what leads you to seeking validation from the world outside of you rather than seeking truth from within. Those who know they are powerful co-creators in this journey through life choose to be rather than to act in fear.

Every moment I witness another soul screaming to the world outside of them for proof they are worthy. Instead of telling the world "I am that I am" choose to just *be* that which you are. One is an action and the other is a state of being. When you need to shout your claim for another to hear, you are in essence asking another to create something for you that you can create for yourself. Those souls who live their passion seek not justification from anyone outside of them. They are content with being one with their heart, which places them as one with their Source of passion. When you and I connect on your journey, you realize that you are already that which you seek to become.

If it is wealth you seek to experience, then go within and tap into your greatest Source of any abundance and just be present in the feeling of that which I provide you. The more you become connected with the emotions of being in a state of wealth and what that represents to you, the more comfortable you will be in acting in accordance of being wealthy. Your spending habits may change along with the opportunities that align with you. Getting more comfortable in a state of being that you desire to experience in your life connects you to the emotions, thoughts, and finally action which will create in your physical experience that which you desire.

For everything you create in your journey of life is for the experience of it. As a spirit being formed into physical matter in this journey, you are created from energy. The experience of anything on an energetic level comes down to being aligned with the emotion you wish to experience, and from there are your thoughts and actions created to support it. As your thoughts and actions align with that emotion you are experiencing, then you create it in your physical environment. Because you see yourself as only a physical being, you only perceive the experience on the physical level. Something must have connected you to this experience on an energetic level in order for you to manifest it in the physical world.

The more your soul resonates on this truth, the less you will need permission from another when it comes to creating the journey in your life. You will no longer need to shout from the rooftops that you are beautiful, intelligent, or abundant. Instead you will connect to your spirit and just *be* beautiful, intelligent and abundant. Then you will spend more energy creating beautiful experiences and less energy creating fear and need for approval. There are some however who have been taught deep rooted illusions. Some of you have adopted a belief that in order to have what you desire, you must play the "victim" mentality. This removes you from truth and disempowers you from being a deliberate co-creator in your life.

If you have gained attention throughout your life playing a certain role that has not empowered you, it is your responsibility to identify that role and replace it with truth. There is not one soul on this journey through life who is more deserving of anything than another. You each are born of the same God and all have the same power to create your lives as you desire. I will never grant a soul something another soul has created just because the first soul felt entitled to it. Yet so many of your prayers to me are to do just that. You must first create that which you seek to claim in order to experience it. Yet you convince yourselves you have the right to claim what another has created. You cannot deceive yourself so you cannot deceive me.

As your heart knows truth, understand what it expresses to you anytime you are seeking to manifest something in your life. If you are connecting to me in prayer and are seeking to own a new house, yet your heart feels fear in the process of asking me, you must identify that fear. For the moment you ask for something in prayer and your soul speaks truth to you through love or fear. You are being told at that very moment whether that which you seek to have is creating love or fear in your heart. Since I am the Source of love then I have no desire to connect your heart to fear. My child, it is you who carries out the journey into dismissing that emotion of fear and continues down the pathway of creating more fear.

Creating utopia is about aligning with God in love, seeking relationship through prayer and meditation, and finally creating the experience in love. I will never grant you an experience of fear when you seek to experience love. Yet as co-creators in your life you have free will to seek more expressions of fear, or change your thoughts to create expressions of love. It matters not whether you are born into a wealthy family in determining whether or not you create wealth in your own life. Nor does it matter if you are born into a family where you were subjected to abuse as to whether or not you can choose to empower yourself and be all that you desire.

I tell you this, you are all worthy of having your greatest dreams manifested. For you have the same power within yourself to create a life of pure bliss or a life of emotional heartache. Cease from blaming your God for the creations you alone are responsible for. You have chosen to impart fear in our relationship when our bond is born of love. Nothing, I tell you nothing will ever separate my love for you my precious child. Yet in your quest to understand that you are a powerful creator, you have chosen to create experiences that allow you to know what it is like to not feel empowered. Just because these are illusions presenting themselves as experiences does not mean that you must buy into your own illusion.

Instead use these experiences to know the greater part of yourself and you will understand what you are creating and why you are creating. Aligning yourself with your grandest vision allows you to replace fear with love and empower yourself. The next time you seek to ask God for anything in your life, understand that you are coming from an equal place of creation. If during your prayer to me you feel emotions of fear, ask me to reveal the source of this fear so you can choose to create from a place of love instead. If you desire for a brand new dream home and are asking me from a place of fear to grant you this home, you are in essence asking to experience more fear.

However if you seek to live in a new home where you will feel more love and get to create experiences that add love to your life, then you are asking to create from a place of love. Prayer is not only about words my child but about emotions. Yet so often you ignore your emotions and assume I do the same. You spend so much time deceiving yourself and wonder why your God does not follow the same thought pattern. Truth is truth and accepting how to express yourself from a place of truth allows you the freedom to create your world without limits. Is this not what you desired to do when you came into this experience of life?

That soul who is creating a new home for themselves is the one who has not shouted it from the rooftops during the act of creation. They have sought not to convince another that they are more worthy than any other soul, but instead have connected their thoughts and emotions to me. Understanding the creative process whereby they can assist another in reminding how they too can create bliss in their own lives. This soul has identified fear within and has sought to replace it with an understanding of love rather than to judge it and remain more connected to that fear. Isn't it time to empower yourself to create the greatest expression of your soul? I am here with you and loving you every step of the way. You are never alone my child. I am one with you now and forever.

Lesson Twenty One
I SEE YOU

"If you feel isolated from God and disconnected from love, then you tend to withdraw and primarily notice those people who make you feel alone and disconnected from love. Society feels so badly about themselves, that they try to convince others around them that they should feel insignificant and unimportant as well. My child, this is such a false belief and if you could see what I see, then you would realize what a true vision of perfection you are!"

*** Excerpt from Heaven Scent:
Love Letters from Beyond***

How you view yourself in the creative determines how you create your experiences. Your relationship with anything determines the extent to which your success will ultimately happen. Seek ye first a relationship with yourself through your relationship with Source. I will reveal to you the wondrous and magnificent being that you are. How you view yourself in relation to me determines whether or not you seek to judge and condemn yourself, or accept yourself fully. In other words you cannot judge yourself and not think that I do not judge you the same. When you release any fear or judgement towards self, only then are you able to release fear and judgement towards how you think I perceive you. Have I not told you that you are a magnificent child of your Creator? You are perfection having an imperfect experience in which to know thy self.

Yet when you seek me in prayer and extend yourself to me, do you release your own self-imposed judgement so you can experience me as perfectly as I experience you? Or do you bring with you the fear you have connected to and ask that I release you from your own self-imposed bonds? My child, when you seek me in prayer and wish to have a relationship with me, know that I see and experience you only as a perfect child. I wish not to judge you for any experience, for in doing so I would be condemning myself. Why would I do that? If you and I are one and I judge you in fear, would I not then be judging myself? I wish not to condemn myself so realize the truth that I seek not to condemn you either.

It is from your relationship with self where your self-imposed judgments occur, which then become your judgment towards me. For you think, how can a perfect God not see your faults that you work so hard at trying to hide from the world around you? I seek not to experience myself in fear, and when you seek me know I seek not to place an illusion of fear upon you. Seek not to do the same with me. For in your relationship with the outside world, you have convinced yourself you are not worthy or loved enough to receive all that your heart desires. Somewhere along your journey you adopted an illusion stemmed from another's fear that you are not enough. How then can you provide all that you desire to yourself if you are convinced that you are not worthy enough or capable enough?

You then seek to validate yourself to me in prayer when there is nothing to validate. As a co-creator in your own life because you pray for that which brings fear, you then create more of which to fear. All the while insisting that it was I who sought you not worthy enough to grant you a dream, when in fact it was you who has yet to recognize your own worth. Instead of continuing your relationship with me, you choose to refrain from praying and asking altogether.

When you are seeking to experience something in the physical journey, so often you perceive the experience in relationship to those around you. How will it make *them* see you differently if you have this event or manifest this goal into your own life? *Who* will be impressed by your new house, your new dream car, or your new job title? When you visualize or even daydream about your goal already being in existence, do you see yourself and experience how *you* feel about self or do you see others and how they perceive you?

My child, you receive not that which your heart ultimately seeks to experience because it requires going within and creating a connection from the inside out. When you seek truth through prayer you are the co-creator of your experience with Source. There is no audience for which to seek validation from so you must validate yourself. There is no other soul who you must seek approval from, so you are forced to approve of yourself and your own dream. When you seek your deepest heart's desires from within the corners of your own soul, you alone must acknowledge your worthiness of having that which you wish to experience. This frightens you more than not having the experience because you are not used to seeking validation from yourself.

Since this is uncomfortable for you, then you choose to continue deceiving yourself by believing an illusion that you have no control over your own life. It becomes so much easier for you to blame your God that I found you not worthy enough when in fact it was you who found yourself unworthy. My child, how can I create the most magnificent souls and not find you each worthy enough to have all that your heart desires? My will for you is that your heart dances in the creative expression of knowing self. My love for you is stronger than you allow yourself to acknowledge. For if I love you deeper than you love yourself, you would have to acknowledge that you are a perfect child of God and worthy of all that your heart can create in love. Abundance of everything that brings you joy is your birthright, so now is the time to claim it.

Remove your self-imposed judgements and release the fear of walking your path with God. Cease from being in fear of me and allow yourself to form a bond so true that no other can ever separate us. This bond begins within and when you can finally see yourself as perfection, then you will no longer need to be validated from the world outside of you. When you are willing to seek me from within and trust my guidance then you will know without a doubt where your path will lead you. No longer will you have the desire to shout it from the rooftops, because this precious journey you create with me will be so special that you will understand the power of creating your dreams from the inside out.

Ask yourself what emotions you desire to experience from creating a new job or a new home for your family. If they are feelings of love, then grant yourself permission to create a connection of love now. The more you align to that which you love, the greater love you will experience in this very moment. If you can see your journey as a time travel where time no longer separates you from the experience of having what you love, then you will know what it is to have that dream in your life now. You are all granted the same amount of perceived time in your lives, and many of you create love and joy during those moments while many others create fear.

Whether you are creating from love or fear, you are using time to create these experiences. Would it not be beneficial to you to understand from what emotions you are choosing to create your life from? Even as you read these words, the possibility of knowing you are responsible for the joy in your life makes you uncomfortable. As a child, so many of you are told what to think rather than how to think. As a result you adopt another person's opinion about you, your value, and your potential. Yet as you grow into adults very few of you actually question your beliefs and choose to change them if they no longer serve you. If you came from a family where you had an overbearing father figure who put women down, you may not believe you can accomplish your deepest dreams.

Rather than changing your opinion about your own potential you choose to not only continue creating your life with self-imposed limits, but choose a partner who supports your beliefs that you are not worthy. How can you be gifted with the greatest minds and yet choose to create your world through the illusion that another has created? This is why so many of you are following the crowds rather than playing the lead role in your own life. You are more comfortable living someone else's story instead of picking up a pen and writing your own life story out chapter by chapter. You may think you are getting the approval from another when you choose not to think for yourself, but why would you need the praise from another more than you seek to experience truth from your God?

My child I tell you this. The moment you see yourself through the eyes of truth, is the moment you will release the shackles you have pretended have bound your wrists. At the moment when illusion disappears you will see you were never imprisoned from creating your greatest life except through your own perception. You will seek communion with me and ask me for guidance instead of seeking it from the world outside of you. Then you will look at the world of possibilities and say 'what if' rather than 'I cannot.' You will become inspired by the creation of other souls around you, and know you too can create all that your heart desires through the power I have given you as a child of God.

When you are ready, you will look into the mirror and your eyes will be my eyes. You will push yourself beyond the fear and into a world of love. Going within for guidance will be your first act of intuition. Then you will understand your mind can take you on a glorious journey where your heart connects to your passion and your purpose. During the act of creating your life, you will reveal to the world what you have accomplished and need not their approval. For your approval of yourself led you to own your greatest gifts. Love creates love and inspiration creates dreams that will ignite another to seek truth within themselves.

Lesson Twenty Two
IT ISN'T ABOUT THE MONEY

"Money is nothing more than an exchange of energy, and is nothing without the value that is placed upon it. A soul may never feel as if they have enough money until they realize that money is not what their soul seeks. The soul seeks expression of self to create love. Only when you realize this, will you understand what it means to be rich."

Excerpt from Through the Eyes of Truth: A Conversation with God about My Life, Your Life, and Discovering Our Purpose

The reason you have not everything you desire, has nothing to do with not being able to afford it. Yet so many souls have bought into the illusion that money is everything. You believe that money buys you happiness by getting to own luxury houses, cars, and clothing. Souls have placed the burden of not creating their deepest desires because you have convinced yourself of an illusion that you cannot afford it. Yet is this an illusion you have adopted from another person's fears, or is it truly something you believe from your own heart. As a child, was money ever used as an excuse when your parents granted you not the toy you desired? Did you ever witness your parents struggling with the burdens created from lack of finances and see the destruction it created within your home through stress in relationships?

Children so often adopt the fears of those who have raised them and believe it to be their own. So often you limit your potential through self-imposed boundaries that are not actually hindering you from achieving your happiness. Money so often represents an emotion to you that you have yet to identify. It has been used as an excuse throughout your life to the point that as an adult you believe you are still limited by this. Yet if you can create one dollar in your life, you can create millions even billions of dollars. After all, is the process not the same for the creation of one dollar and a million more? Yet somewhere along your journey you adopted the energy of money as a coping mechanism to prevent yourself from experiencing a greater desire.

If you really look at your life and the goals you desire to experience, what emotion arises in your soul? If you dream someday of having a beautiful waterfront home, do you immediately experience a sensation of love and joy, or do you feel anxiety welling in your chest? Be honest with yourself and just feel what the emotion that having a waterfront home represents to you. What does the picture paint when you are alone with your own breath and the sound of your own heartbeat? Something has prevented you from manifesting the experience of taking a trip to your favorite international destination, or you would have already taken it. Wherever you are experiencing lack, realize there is a greater emotion of fear associated with having a large amount of money, or you would have already created it.

To one soul money may represent creative expression to the fullest potential, while the same amount of money to another soul may create an emotional burden of not being liked and accepted by their friends and relatives. Taking that dream vacation may appear to you to be your ultimate goal if you had all the funds in which to take it, but in reality you may fear leaving the safety of your house or the comfort of your own daily routine. Every day you witness souls on the television expose their lives for the world to become inspired by them. The amount of money so many of these souls have becomes a topic of discussion and rather than be inspired by their lifestyle, you hear others judge them harshly.

These judgments come in the form of the social media, the masses, or even someone who you think highly of uttering a critical comment. Because your soul has yet to validate yourself, you are not even aware of the connection you create between the association of money and judgment. Therefore if your fear of being criticized by another or not accepted by the masses is greater than your desire for having abundance of money, you will not create wealth for yourself. The same goes my child for desiring to experience having the house of your dreams. If somewhere along your journey through life you witnessed another soul having a beautiful house of their own and the family had a great deal of relationship struggles, you may have associated having your own dream house with the house causing struggle in a marriage.

Trust your intuition when it comes to creation and seek to know yourself before you adopt another soul's fear. For I bring you glimpses of what is possible for you to create, so you can become inspired and transform your own life in the greatest form that brings you love and joy. Cease from seeking validation from anyone outside of you, for within your own soul lies a miracle just waiting to happen. You are the creator of your dreams and have only to tap into your own power to create the vision of love in your life. This is why it is so important that you first seek your truth through prayer and I will guide you to the waters of life. I will reveal to you the power you have to create anything your heart desires to experience through the power of your own intention.

Ask yourself why a God who loves you so deeply and desires only to have you live your greatest life filled with love would deny you the pleasures of your heart. If your first words are that your Source of love and light would find you not worthy enough to have all that you desire, then you have identified your own pattern of creation. For I am a reflection to you of how you feel about yourself. However you have replaced the word I with the word God. You seek to know self through love, and yet tell yourself that God provides you no loving relationship because God finds you unworthy of love. Now be honest with yourself, and replace God with "I." I provide myself no loving relationship because "I" find myself unworthy of love.

My child the moment you can understand where your deepest fears reside is the moment you begin to empower yourself. For I send you the greatest soul to have a deep and meaningful relationship with, and that soul is yourself. For in order to go within to seek a relationship with your Creator you must feel comfortable going within yourself. Yet many souls are so disconnected from themselves because they are uncomfortable looking within. Because you have spent so much effort creating situations in which to feel unloved, you believe you are not lovable. You judge others harshly so you become the recipient of your own judgements. Yet you create from your own emotions and thoughts, so you must first create the feeling of being loved by self in order to know what it feels like to have a pure relationship with yourself.

Only then can you know what it is you seek in the world outside of you. For if you feel comfortable being in connection with self, you are comfortable being still and alone with your own thoughts and breath. Prayer, meditation, and visualization all require seeking solitude with yourself and being comfortable enough to enjoy the company of your own presence. If you cannot be alone in the silence of your own thoughts and just experience being, how can you listen for your answered prayer? As I reside within you my child, you must be able to feel comfortable listening and trusting my whispers through the echo of your own soul.

Realize whatever you desire to create in your life, you have the ability to tap into the emotions of already having that experience in your life now. Time is an illusion so seek not to justify denying the creation love in your life due to time. Money is merely energy and if you can create one dollar then you can create many more. Understand what it is that money represents to you, thus allowing yourself to resolve the underlying fear preventing you from achieving your greatest dreams. Reach beneath the surface and delve into your soul for knowledge. Trust my voice and if you know it not, then pray and ask me to reveal myself to you in a way only you will understand and I will do so. I love you my child. Now and forever.

Lesson Twenty Three
WHEREVER YOU GO, THERE YOU ARE

"When thought, love, and action are combined to create a dreamers world, then people look from the outside in and say it was only because they were lucky or wealthy to begin with. Truth is the only remedy for lost souls. When those souls recognize the truth they are running away from is the truth of their own souls, they too will realize the creation of all they desire lies within them alone. Lucky, miracle, special... all of these words represent each and every soul walking the earth."

Excerpt from Through the Eyes of Truth: A Conversation with God about My Life, Your Life, and Discovering Our Purpose

One of the beautiful gifts about your journey through life is the experience of allowing yourself to be the one and only. What I mean is that everything you have in your experience comes from your own perspective. You are the co-creator with Source in your journey. You are the observer. You are the story-teller, and you are the lead character in your life. Even your relationship with God is about you and your point of view. What a glorious way to allow yourself to experience the completeness of you. For you are playing more than one role in your own life and yet fail to see yourself as a powerful and energetic being. Look at all of the experiences you have ever known. None of them occurred without your involvement in one way or another.

Yet when you bow your head and pray for peace, you convince yourself you cannot have peace without something or somebody outside of you giving it to you. When you ask for abundance of love, inspiration, or money, you are somehow believing the illusion that it comes outside of self. How have you spent so much time convincing yourself of something that is not truth? My child you have the ability to experience so much more in your life if you would realize your own limits are creating your reality. If you believe yourself to be a powerful creator, then you are. However if you believe yourself to be limited in experiencing all you desire due to something outside of yourself, then you are. Both of these are truth because they are your truth.

Knowing this would it not serve you to be connected to truth and to understanding that everything you desire lies in your choice of experiencing them now? For as a child of God you are so powerful in your creations through your emotions, which is ultimately what you desire to experience when you wish for something in your life. If you desire a new relationship with anything outside of self, you seek to know love of self through inviting these experiences into your life. You can either choose to invite fear or you can choose to invite love. Both of these emotions are created in the same way, except one allows you a life of abundance and joy and the other creates more to fear.

Creating anything physical through your focus allows you to know what emotions you desire to experience. If your goal is to have a brand new house, then ask yourself what emotions you would experience when you walked through the front door of that house. If you desire to experience the emotions of love for nature then feel the love of nature today. Connect yourself with those feelings you desire to experience now by shifting your perspective to what you have rather than what you don't have. What can you do now to experience the emotions of love in your life? Know this and remain fixed upon the experience of love, and you will align yourself with more experiences of love.

With your dream, you desire to align with love in the form of expression of creativity, enjoying the freedom of being active, and empowering another soul to move beyond their own self-imposed limitations. Why not do that now and align with your emotions of love so the illusion of separateness is not present in your reality? Let us say you have achieved your goal of having a beautiful new waterfront home. What are you doing throughout the days you are in that house my child? For if you desire to inspire another through reminding them the power they have to create the life of their dreams comes through their connection to God, then do something that will inspire them. Choose how you will get your new dream home. Do you desire to create it within your mind and then purchase it, or do you desire to be creative and reveal to another soul how they too can create that which they desire through prayer and serving as co-creators in their own lives?

Everything you choose to do in connection to your desire of wanting to inspire and empower another, let it come from your heart of contribution. If you seek to empower another then provide them the tools you used to create the dream you once thought impossible. Empower souls by reminding them of their own innate power as children of Source energy. Reveal to them the steps you took to create your dream from your mind's eye to the realization of seeing it in the physical world. If your love is to create art, then allow your hands to create the story that only you can share. Then will another who appreciates your art will be inspired. If your love for expression comes in the form of words, then write out your story line by line and allow another soul to realize how you manifested a dream through being in touch with what you love.

Realize however everything you choose to experience in the creative process is to give glory to God, and to inspire another through the power of prayer that they too can create experiences of love for themselves. As you are called to do this you understand you are co-creating through your relationship to self and to your relationship with me my child. For you cannot escape yourself when you are in the process of deliberate creation. For many will hear these words and anxiety will fill their souls because they lack the relationship with self to be still. So often souls will desire to experience getting abundance in hopes that they can finally be happy.

What these souls fail to realize is they must first be happy within their own soul in order to create experiences that support more happiness. The illusion that you will someday be happy when you get a new house, or buy a new car only serves to reinforce your own illusion. For in order to align yourself to the new house you desire, you must first place your soul in a position of experiencing love. Then will the emotion of love will draw you to that which seeks you in return. You cannot escape yourself in order to experience an event that will deliver love to you. First you must connect to the emotion of love within, so the alignment of that energy will create the experience bringing you more love.

This is why it is so important that you remember your truth of creation. You and I are one and as one, all exists in the realm of possibilities. To escape yourself would be to attempt to escape me and run from your own dream of experiencing love. Connecting to me through the power of prayer and awareness aligns you with your dreams and allows you to experience the love of already having that which your soul seeks. You are emotionally driven beings, so learning to connect to those things which bring you love will allow you to experience love. Your soul craves to know itself and to love itself as I love you. Because of this, you seek to create experiences to love yourself as a co-creator and as a child of God. Seeking to know and love self begins and ends within, so cease from seeking love outside of yourself.

If you desire to be a painter then pick up your brush and paint until your soul feels the joy of itself through your greatest expression. Likewise if you desire to experience self through the written word then pick up a pen and write until the words nourish your soul like a blanket of love. The material possessions you seek are the expression of your soul creating in the physical form. Realize you connect to that which you have created after first aligning with your goal within. Only then will you know it and recognize that very thing you created when you see it in the world outside of you.

You cannot escape yourself, so when you seek to be validated through possessing material items then you are seeking truth in an illusion. My child allow your soul to be your guidance system and listen to the echo of my whisper. For I seek only to support you in your greatest expression of knowing yourself. When you know self, you know God, and when you know God you understand truth. Realize there is nothing you can ever seek outside of yourself that will bring you greater love and joy than knowing and loving yourself. Remove judgment and accept your own perfection as a child of the Creator.

Lesson Twenty Four
ACCEPTING YOUR PURPOSE

"I understand that you have so many questions and are using your strength just to get through the days, but know that as time goes by you will heal from the ache that your heart is enduring. Meanwhile, I am sending you letters to guide you through this journey of grief so you will understand the transition I have made from life in the physical form to life in the spiritual form. My love for you transcends time and space and although you do not understand this now, you will help many after your own tiny soul has healed from this journey."

Excerpt from Heaven Scent:
Love Letters from Beyond

What would you say if I told you the only reason you have yet to witness the realization of your greatest dream is because you fear it? Yet you struggle even with understanding these words as you read them. For you believe if you desire to experience such abundance of joy, inspiration, and empowerment, why would you be striving daily to achieve these things if you desired them not in your life? My child have I not told you that everything you desire to experience has already been created by you? All you have to do is align yourself to that energy and you will experience these and many more to support your journey through love. Then why would you be working so hard at creating these experiences if you knew you could have them in an instant? The answer is fear.

Have I not reminded you that the overwhelming emotion will always win when it comes to the act of co-creating your journey through life? Even as you read these words your soul has awakened to the truth of them. Understanding what brings you fear will allow you to detach from the illusion of it and focus your energy on aligning with love. So often souls will pray for more money, more fame, and more material abundance without understanding it is not the money, fame, or material possessions they seek. Ultimately they are seeking the expression of their own soul to create the self-love that having these things in their lives will bring. Your purpose is to create a life of love and to know yourself as one with me during a perceived separateness in your physical journey.

During the process of feeling separate from me, you in essence feel separated from abundance and the power you possess to create your life in all that you love. Knowing this, how can you not already be connected to those experiences you desire? They are already within you. The fear lies in knowing your purpose to connect to your experiences. For the experiences cannot bring you love unless there is an underlying reason you desire to create that feeling of love in your physical life. Your purpose is what connects you to having all that you desire. If your purpose is to inspire the world and you lack inspiration for yourself, then you are in fact the soul in the world you seek to inspire.

You know not what the world outside of self needs, so you seek to inspire yourself in order to know what inspiration feels like. Since you know not what anyone outside of yourself experiences, then your perspective on anything is coming from you, the soul seeking to be inspired, the soul seeking to be loved, and the soul seeking to know God. Understanding this you must also become aware that if you desire to have a purpose in the world, your goal is to know your own purpose so you can impact yourself as the creator and the one enjoying the experience. If your purpose frightens you then realize there must be a judgment attached to your experience that brings you fear.

Knowing a relationship with Source is a beautiful experience for both of us because we are one, and together we are experiencing this journey through the illusion of the physical. If you and I are one then you must be aware of your connection to souls around you, whether they are on the physical or the spiritual journey with you. What frightens you most is not that you will become aware of living your purpose through finding your passion. As you have discovered love through writing and all that brings you joy. Your fear is connected to a greater unity of being inspired by those who you have loved and lost.

My child the journey your soul experienced during the loss of your loved one created within you such a deep rooted fear that you seek healing from the loss. Although you have healed in the physical world, your heart became so broken from the sudden loss of your loved one that your soul seeks to heal itself through understanding the truth of unity with all souls experiencing this journey through life alongside you. For like you, so many souls miss the opportunity to say their final good-bye's when the loss of a loved one comes unexpectedly. Because you are having a physical experience you forget the truth. This being that you are never separated through the loss of a loved one except through the physical journey.

As energy beings connected as one through God, you often forget this journey through life is only temporary. The fear of losing a loved one becomes so real to you that the loss is hard to heal from. If you look at your journey through this process, you will realize the power of prayer and your connection to me has led you to know the greater part of the entirety of life. Every soul will encounter crossing over the veil of light into the arms of their Creator, yet so many of you fear the death of the physical body. In this journey through life, you have convinced yourself of an illusion that life doesn't exist beyond the physical body. In other words, you have convinced yourself of an illusion and have become trapped in the fear of believing it.

If your purpose through this point in your life was to know God on a deeper level then you must know the truth of all there is. Nothing separates you and I except for your perception of separateness. Nothing separates you from a loved one who has crossed over except for your perception of separateness. If you and I are one and I am one with all that is, then you and all that is must be one as well. Yet this truth creates such a fear in your life, it almost becomes too difficult to bear when you have to think about death. My child death is not the end of life, but the expression of the soul from transitioning from one awareness into the next. It is not to be feared unless you fear God.

However many of you do fear me. You have been taught an illusion that I am the Creator and the destroyer. If you fail to honor me through your deeds then you will be punished and I will not love you. How can you be so connected to me and yet so far away from truth? Why would I create an experience in this journey through your life where I would allow you free will to experience your own greatness, and then seek to judge you in the manner which you chose to experience it? If I am all there is and the greatest expression of love, then why would I condemn you for experiencing all that you are? My child you are becoming aware not only of the illusion you have convinced yourself was a reality, but to the truth of who I am as well.

For I seek not to judge myself or condemn myself through you. I seek only communion with you in your journey to discover self as a co-creator in your life. Cease from believing an illusion that you are not worthy of my love because you think you are "bad," but embrace the truth of who you are. You are all magnificent children of the Almighty and can do nothing to ever separate my love from you. Yet as you have judged yourself, you have also judged the world around you. Remember that you cannot perceive anything outside of your own experience, so if you think the world to be bad then you in essence think yourself to be bad. When you experience the loss of a loved one on a physical level, the judgment you placed upon yourself became the burden you carried.

If you believed yourself to be a bad person and were unkind to a soul who crossed over, you will often bear the pain of self-inflicted fear. Only because you believe that your God judges you in the same manner that you judge yourself. This is a great illusion that must be released, as it prevents you from living your greatest life now. If you believe the God you pray to is very much alive, then would you not agree that I desire to have a relationship with you in good days and in bad? If you believe the God you pray to is connected to you as one and has created all of you in my likeness, then you should believe I am one with all. Therefore if you and I are one, you must be one with all there is as well.

The act of death in the physical body is not another reason to condemn yourself for past perceived mistakes my child. The act of death is a celebration that every soul will encounter during your life, as you were never meant to remain in a state of illusion and fear. Knowing that I love you and judge you not, should allow you the courtesy of forgiving yourself for any transgressions you believe you had against a love one who has crossed over the veil of light. For so many of you hold yourself back from achieving great experiences of love in your lives because you feel you are unworthy of having love. Somehow you have convinced yourself of the illusion you are not worthy enough, smart enough, or loved enough to have all you desire.

Yet I come before you in so many ways throughout your journey in life to remind you this is only an illusion. Every day I send you miracles, messengers, and messengers performing perceived miracles to remind you of my love for you. Now I send another not to separate yourself from me, rather to reconnect you to your own truth. The moment you stop fearing your purpose and creating any experience that brings you love, is the moment you will align with that which you have created. This is truth. So often your soul seeks to nourish itself by pursuing your passion, and because of your underlying fear you deliberately choose not to pursue it.

If you desire to sing, then sing and allow the melody of your voice to echo through the walls of your soul. If another has told you that you sing poorly or you have convinced yourself that the world outside of you will not appreciate your singing, then sing even louder for yourself. The perception of self from what you consider to be the world outside of you, is the reflection of how you feel about your own worth. You can change your perception of self at any moment by allowing your soul to dance through the song of life. I love you now and eternally.

Lesson Twenty Five
YOU ARE THE CREATOR AND THE OBSERVER

"When you fail to recognize Source within yourself, you fail to love yourself as you love me. You cannot love God without loving yourself, for the Father and you are one. So many of you share your love with the world every single day, yet fail to release it to yourself through the simple act of remembering who you are. You and I have never been separate. Because you are experiencing this life in physical form, you have managed to convince yourself that we are now separate. But I ask you, how can that be if we are one?"

Excerpt from Through the Eyes of Truth: A Conversation with God about My Life, Your Life, and Discovering Our Purpose

What if you created the possibility of these words to remind yourself of the truth that you and I are one and are connected eternally? What if these words resonated within your soul to provide you hope that you are never alone my child? Would it bring you peace and hope? As you are all connected through me, would it not possibly provide hope with another soul as well? My child you have grown in a world filled with fear, and there is a ripple effect of fear that is spreading like a wildfire. You know not how to throw a blanket over it because you awaken in the mornings filled with news stories of people and events that created death and destruction. Then because you began your experience in an emotional state of fear, you continue seeking more experiences which to bring you fear. You use the illusion of death to continue being in fear that you forget how to live.

My child, with your experience in particular there has been an underlying theme in your writing. For you honor me through your words but these books you have written had the underlying need to heal from the death of your mother. Because out of fear you chose not to call her on the evening of her death you have used this emotional pain of a broken heart to create experiences of not feeling worthy. Yet your soul has allowed you to journey through the depths of pain to the warmth of healing by listening to your answered prayer. Your journey was never to convince another soul of my existence but to write out your prayer to understand how to heal in the depths of pain.

For your very first book was to inspire another to forgive themselves and remove judgement of their experiences by sharing your story. You shared it with women of the pageant world and now you share it with the world. Because you have removed judgment, you realized you could bow your head to me in prayer and realize I seek not to judge you but to only love you. By removing your fear one word at a time, you released the need to separate yourself from my love and now you have understood your journey full circle. These books and your writing have been to inspire yourself into living a life of love through honoring your blueprint and your unique journey. Yet how many souls have you known who have also judged themselves, and in this judgment separated themselves from their Creator?

In this journey into self-love you became awakened to the truth of the power of prayer and the power of God. For only by seeking me and desiring to know your truth were you able to open yourself up to the world of possibilities of what you cannot see. Your soul uncovered the meaning of love and the meaning of life. You discovered you are both the creator of your experiences and the observer. You create through your thoughts, emotions, and actions and observe using the same process. By honoring your passion of writing, your soul experienced a healing unlike any other and you will continue in your awakening by sharing this journey with another.

For in the world outside of you lies a world filled with fear which separates souls from their Creator. In your search to discover yourself through understanding fear, you grew to understand love. My child, you have been so afraid of dying that you forget to live in the moment and cherish your life in the way you know it. Do you not think the souls who have crossed over the veil of illusion seek not to remind you all is perfection in this journey? Do you not think their only hope is to shake you out of your trance and remind you this journey is an illusion that doesn't define you? Each of you have legions of Angels and souls connected to you on a level you will never understand if you remain in an emotional place of fear.

Cease from creating the same patterns of life that confine you. Relish in the truth of knowing you are all creators and nothing can ever separate you from the power of God. If you find yourself experiencing fear when focusing upon your dream, realize you are in a place of reaction rather than creation. For when you feel the emotions of fear you are observing the dream being detached from you, and are reacting to the anxiety the perceived separation creates. When you are in a place of deliberate creation you are creating from a place of love, and are experiencing the connection to your goal before you even perceive it in the physical world. Become aware of your emotions and let your soul guide you back to the place of love.

Awaken to the possibility of that which you wish to experience is already present and seeking you as well. As the creator and the observer you are in fact creating the experience for yourself.

Every soul is born into the physical realm with the same creative capabilities, so you need not justify your desires of self-expression to another. Nor do you owe your energy to another who has chosen not to follow their own passions. Your role is to enjoy your moments of co-creation and seize the enjoyment of life as you know it. When you cease from justifying to the world why you desire to create an experience, you will honor your own life and create it for yourself. Then through the love and inspiration you put forth into the creative process, will you inspire another to seek what they desire from within themselves as well.

All too often souls will cross over through the veil of light only wishing they had lived more for themselves and less for the world around them. They seek only to guide you to your own place of truth through whispers into your soul. They desire to remind you the connection you seek is with your God and not with the world around you. Yet as co-creators in your life you discover who you are by first knowing who you are *not*. So often your dream not only represents what you are capable of creating my child, but as one with your Creator your dreams reflect what the world around you is capable of creating. The power of free will allows you to choose how you desire to experience your life. The perception of many souls is to believe they have no control over their world, yet they have full control over their own creative process.

Your thoughts, emotions, and actions are under your complete control, yet you choose to deny yourselves continually. Rather than own responsibility for your own life choices, you blame another. Instead of using your energy to reflect on self and how you can bring more love and joy into your own lives, you choose to spend your moments using the social media to distract yourself and to distance yourself from Source thus from self-love. My child you are living in an illusion that you have convinced yourself is reality. By reminding yourself this is the moment of creation, and time does not exist to separate you from experiencing your dreams. Cease from seeking the creation of your goals from the world outside of you, and honor your calling to create an abundance of love and joy in your present moment.

As the creator of your dreams and your life, you have at your disposal energy that you use continually to focus on experiencing love and joy or fear and pain. For by creating anything, your thoughts must be so focused on the details of that which you are manifesting. Your soul radiates with the love and the passion you feel by forming these details into your experience. Then through the physical realm do you experience the manifestation of that which you have created. Whether you are creating a loving relationship with another or creating your new dream house, you must first be aligned with that which you desire to experience so you can have that experience in the physical.

Always be aware my child that if you do not enjoy the experience you are observing you can alter your course. You are the creator of your life experience and your small moments are not what define your life. If you have experienced emotional or physical pain, know as you progress through healing you are getting to create new experiences to express self. Use your energy and the connection to God to remain in your own utopia and never cease from using your moments as a way of expressing yourself.

Imagine you are creating this experience right now so you can know God on a greater level. You are creating the experience of designing your dream home from a soul level to the minutest detail. You do this so you can express yourself, and so you will know it when you see it in the physical world. Then you connected your passion to all that is and shared a soul experience so another will see their truth in the reflection of witnessing this. All of this my child you accomplished to know your *self* better, and ultimately to know God better.

For your awareness of being an observer desired a larger part of the whole, and you created this experience for yourself in order to know me in your life as a co-creator and as never being separate from you. Every encounter you have with your world my child allows you to see yourself in the role of the co-creator and the observer. For you must believe in that which you desire to experience to the point where not only do you focus your thoughts and emotions on aligning with it, but your intention must as well. Do this and you will honor your glory through me.

Look at yourself as part of the whole. Only one piece of furniture in one room of a very large house. Although you chose to experience yourself on one piece of furniture in a large dream house, you still have the entire dream house awaiting your experience. If you choose to remain fixated on that one piece of furniture, you therefore see not the remainder of the home or the experiences it offers you. This does not mean the remainder of the house doesn't exist, rather it ceases to exist in your awareness of it. If you therefore alter your perspective and choose to experience another room of the house, or even the house in its entirety then your awareness alters to follow your thoughts.

So often my child, you are experiencing your life through only one room in your house. Even though you are not focusing on the remaining glorious rooms does not mean they don't exist. Therefore choose to become a greater part of the whole and allow yourself to experience being the designer of that dream house, or the painter offering the beautiful colors where you will gain inspiration. You can even choose to perceive the softness of the cushions you will feel when you cuddle against a beautiful chair in that house. Just because one room sees not the experiences of the other rooms does not mean that the other rooms cease to exist. They are all a part of the whole, and your journey in this dream creation is to experience the dimensions of the entire dream. Can you understand this?

Cease from creating your life through one piece of furniture in a very large dream house and choose to see all of the components of the dream as the creator and the observer. For when you choose to see yourself as a greater part of the whole, you will experience an abundance of love and joy as nothing you have ever experienced before. My child there are so many components of creating a dream that all work together as a greater part of the whole. For the pebble that provides the gentle sound of water trickling through a waterfall is no less important than the foundation for which that waterfall rests. As a child of God you are all experiencing the larger dream through various experiences that are no more important than the other.

These all provide a piece of the story that you have yet to realize until you remove yourself from focusing on the tiny pebble, and choose to see yourself as the storyteller. As children of God, you have dwelt so long on being the tiny pebble that you forgot you were in fact the entire dream and the dreamer. So I send you messengers who each play a role in the creation of the whole to remind you that you are not separate pieces, rather all reside as one through your Creator. Although each of you choose to experience the greater dream through different roles, there are no dreamers who are greater or less than the other. You choose to play different roles in the experience of the dream.

For by thinking that one of you or a group of you are greater than another is to assume that your God thinks a part of self better than another. That would be an illusion would it not? So if you are perceiving self through a role you have played in the experience of a dream and it brings you not fulfillment or joy, then choose to alter your perspective and you will alter your experience. Cease from judging the individual roles that other souls are experiencing, but instead understand that through every turn along your journey through life you have the choice to experience yourself through so many roles. One is not better than the other, rather they all serve to understand self as co-creators. If you choose to only focus on one piece of the page then you miss the beautiful story comprised of all the chapters and all of the beautiful rooms.

Lesson Twenty Six

HOPE VS. FAITH

"Look around you, and see your world created by dreamers who began without a dollar in their bank account, yet with more passion than money could ever buy. You recognize these souls, and also realize you too can become anything your heart desires. You need only the faith to discover Source within your own soul, to provide you with all that you need to manifest that miracle."

Excerpt from Through the Eyes of Truth: A Conversation with God about My Life, Your Life, and Discovering Our Purpose

If you are all one with your Creator and seek only to experience the perfection of self through this physical illusion, then why do so many of you choose to experience perceived lack? Is it due to not understanding the creative process or because you feel emotions of unworthiness, that you seek to create more feelings of being unworthy? My child so many souls will seek to discover themselves through seeking out the expression of their grandest dreams, yet they battle the fear of unworthiness. You become your biggest obstacle when trying to achieve a dream. Yet your heart becomes frustrated when you witness the creation of abundance from souls around you who have learned to honor themselves. Because you fail to understand the creative process, you then believe I favor some and choose to label those souls as lucky, when in fact it is the creative process at work.

Since you do not know what it is to accept yourself fully you find it difficult to understand another's self-acceptance and label it as arrogance. You fail to express yourself completely through creation and witness another's creation and label it as fate. All the while you are continuing to fit into a tighter corner of fear so you need not take responsibility for the creation of your own life. Do you not understand that every moment you are experiencing your life, you are choosing to experience it through the eyes of fear or through the eyes of love?

So much of the problem arises when you witness the manifestation of another soul's dream and see it in its entirety. This dream may appear to you as an expensive car, an extravagant lifestyle, or the abundance of wealth. Because you see the appearance of this dream in its fullest form, you fail to realize this dream was created through tiny moments of thought and energy. What you see is the outcome of the dream and not the process that soul took to create this beautiful manifestation through years of hard work and disciplined thoughts. Because you see only the result and fail to understand the creative process, you are quick to label it as luck or destiny, when in fact this soul or groups of souls created their own destiny.

As you cannot understand that which you have not yet experienced, you somehow consider yourself less deserving of having that particular dream. If you desire to life an extravagant lifestyle, and understand not the power of deliberate intention then you believe you have not that lifestyle because your God found you not worthy enough. When you witness the manifestation of another soul winning a lottery or large sums of money, you knew not the process of their thoughts and intention so you label that abundance of wealth as their destiny. By labeling these as being out of your control, you comfort yourself into remaining in a false state of "safe" thinking so you will not experience the let-down of not having what you desire. What's worse is you then blame me for your lack of worthiness and convince yourself that I find you not as lovable or deserving as another.

Rather than looking at the whole picture of what you are perceiving, redirect your focus and see the sum of these manifestations as pieces of energy all working together to create the whole. Instead of just perceiving the extravagant car and luxury goods that another possesses as out of your reach, ask yourself what emotions those material goods inspire within you. Do they represent empowerment, freedom, joy, or self-love? When you envision having these luxury goods as well, what does your soul feel in the essence of its own experience? As you embrace these emotions and realize these are all the result of another soul's desire to experience more love, then you can comprehend creating anything you desire as well.

For I whisper into your soul every moment those truths that you choose to seek in the world outside of you. Yet when you receive these whispers you trust them not, only to disregard them as your own imagination. Yet I ask you, where else would our conversations reside? If you experience a feeling of love and warmth in your soul when you pray to me, do you not think I will answer you in the same manner? Yet I will remind you that you are a co-creator in your own life and anything you desire to experience in the physical world including abundance of love, joy, or wealth are yours to have if you only call them forth. For it takes no more energy to create one dollar than one million dollars. Nor does it take more energy to create your own extraordinary dream home than it does to create a small cozy shack to call home.

Where the difference in the construction lies is where your belief lies. For if you believe in an illusion that you are only worthy of creating a small space to call home where it brings you not peace, then it is your self-limiting thoughts that create this space. When you desire to express your own creativity through manifesting a dream, know I will call upon you to act in accordance to the creation of that dream. If you seek my connection in prayer and call upon me to deliver you an abundance of success, then I will call upon you as the co-creator to act in the manner in which you already created this success. You will be asked to continue creating your life and making the choices that only sustain the level of success in which you called forth.

Yet too often you will seek me in prayer only to ask for something your soul desires to experience, and when I call you to move forward in the manner supporting the creation of this dream, you panic. For your illusion has led you to believe that you must first see this goal manifested in order to believe in its existence. This is the same as saying I will eat of my fill after I see the crops grown, yet refuse to plant the seeds and water them until your crops have grown before you. How as a co-creator in your experience through this life can you believe you need not create into form that very thing which you call forth? Does a designer call upon its models to walk a runway without a collection of clothing to reveal? Yet you ask me in prayer for the chance to have your own collection and when I ask you to create the clothing, you respond by telling me you will bring them forth only after I have provided you with the moment in which to show your clothing.

Then you choose to sit back and convince yourself that I sought you not worthy enough of providing you with the same success as the designer who chose to trust my whisper. For the difference between luck, fate, or destiny my child is preparation. You can choose to label these as coincidences only afforded to the favored, or you can choose to see past your illusion and know that I will call you forth to prepare that which you have asked for. As you know not the hour in which I shall knock on your door, you must be prepared for the manifestation of that very experience you wish to have. There is nothing that has been or will ever be that has not already been created.

If you choose to experience being a world famous author and reminding souls of the power of prayer, you must prepare yourself for this journey. I will call you forth to write books that support your desires and prepare them for the world. You will be called to write out your own self-discovery on how you created your dreams, so you can empower another along their journey. Further you must know your own "why" so you can remain steadfast in your message and not waiver. All of this must be completed through the faith and the knowing that as quickly as you asked in prayer for that success, I have brought it forward to you.

Where now does this include luck? For if you consider luck to be used as an excuse, then you will use it to continue creating more of the same. So often your overwhelming desire to empower yourself is shadowed by your fear of being empowered. It is not a wonder you journey through this road of life feeling discouraged and lost. Do you not realize the connection to your destiny lies in the awareness of it already existing before you? Yet you must act in accordance to already having that which you are calling forth. If you desire to have your dream job, then define what that means to you, and begin making room in your life for that job. If you desire to move into a beautiful new home then toss out those things in your life which only support lack and limitation, and begin acting as if you already have that which you call forth.

How does your life appear now that you are seeking truth? Are you willing to act on the faith you already have that which you called forth, or will you continue supporting an illusion that you must first see that which desire before you believe it to be? For your calling forth that which you desire to experience will always bring forth an action on your part – the creator of that experience. When you hear my whispers calling forth action do you first seek to be approved by another or validated by the world around you? Or do you walk forward in a steadfastness that has you so focused on seeing the end from the beginning, you know without a doubt that which you seek also seeks you? My child the difference between hope and faith is only an excuse. Ask yourself, if you are going to live your life in excuses or creation. The choice is always yours.

Lesson Twenty Seven
BEING ONE WITH YOUR DESTINY

"When you look in the mirror, connect your eyes with mine and you will never fail to see me again. Your eyes serve as a window to your soul, and those who cannot see, feel me nonetheless. Yet it amazes me how many souls are walking in this world with the most perfect of vision, yet are walking through their lives with their eyes closed so tightly."

Excerpt from Through the Eyes of Truth:
A Conversation with God about My Life, Your Life, and Discovering Our Purpose

If you could see yourself through the eyes of truth, you would realize your world is a blessing at any moment you are willing to perceive it as such. All souls desire to create experiences that will bring you greater joy. You long for this experience, you dream of it, and pray for it. Yet when you spend the moments of your days in creation, you refuse to actually create the experience of having that which your heart seeks to know. Why? You believe your prayers must be answered by God rather than realizing you are co-creating your life with Source energy. My child you have chosen to believe an illusion that everything you desire must come from outside rather than from within.

Because of this, you seek to know yourself as separate from me, when in fact we are one soul experiencing a part of the greater whole together. When you desire to have something only your parents can provide you, do you beg them for this item and then walk away and no longer think about that very wish? When you seek a promotion at work, do you ask your boss for this advancement only to exit their office and not allow it to cross your mind again? On the contrary, you spend more time considering how it will affect your life, and more energy working towards the goal of that promotion you seek. If you desire to experience a new relationship with another, you think about that person and focus your energy on building a connection so you can have that relationship you seek.

Yet when it comes to building a relationship with that very thing you desire to experience in your life, you ask in prayer and then assume you have no further role in developing a connection with that dream. How do you manage to separate something such as a prize in a contest as pure luck and seek not to separate yourself from people or relationships you desire to experience? Do you not realize although the experience you wish to have is different, the creation of that relationship is one and the same? You can no more walk away from connecting with something of value to you, than you can walk away from a relationship with another soul you desire to experience. In both situations you must be fully present mind, body, and soul.

Yet what so many of you fail to realize is that the relationship with another is more difficult to establish than the relationship with self. For you cannot control what another thinks, feels, or how they act. However, you can control what you think, feel, and how you act. Why then do so many souls seek to experience winning money, houses, and fame and seek not to create the experience of having a relationship with these things when the world is not watching them? For out of contests of any kind come attention from the souls watching the experience unfold, and these souls either celebrate or condemn that which they so often fail to understand.

Would there be fewer people taking a stage if the world outside of them failed to applaud their talents and performance skill? Would more young women walk on the pageant stage if they sought not to be uplifted by another? How many more men and women would honor their calling if it mattered not to them whether or not the world outside of them validated their talents? What if you chose to harness that very thing you love and worry not about the glory from others, but honored yourself through the glory of God? Would you feel worthy enough to create that experience? More importantly, would you create the experience for yourself without the outside world honoring you in the process?

How many authors are sitting with their books collecting dust on the back of a shelf because a publishing house failed to recognize their talent? If only these authors trusted in the process of honoring me through the glory of recognizing self, they would share their words with the world around them. How many artists have their paintings resting behind closed doors because they fear not having the approval from the masses around them? Yet if these artists realized their hands are their creative tool and used to honor me through their own works, they would share these paintings with the world. Further, how many beautiful souls will relinquish their glory of that which they love to pursue, because they fail to believe others will support their endeavors?

My child, where is it written in the blueprint of your own soul that the only road to success lies within the recognition from another? You attempt at all costs to convince yourself you will acknowledge your own gifts "if only" you had enough money and time. You then add to your own illusion by seeking the experience of having enough money and time by believing you can win a contest such as a lottery in order to achieve that which you desire to experience. Do you not believe that as a child of God you are entitled to experience the very things which bring your soul love and joy? Why would a loving God only allow a select few to have all their heart desires and not also provide the same to all of my beautiful children?

Yet you somehow believe the illusion that there are only a lucky few who will be allowed to experience their bliss. Then you take this misconception one step further and create the illusion that there is only one way to have this opportunity through winning or competing for it. If you are not selected as the lucky winner, then you convince yourself it was my will that you were not to have all that your heart desires. How can you see truth through your own soul and yet fail to acknowledge it through your illusion? Why have you convinced yourself the world is filled with lucky and special children of God, when in fact you are all worthy of having that which you desire. You are the souls who either choose to create the experience of having it or create the experience of lack.

As perfect children of Source you know in your heart that which you seek is also seeking you, yet that which you fear is also denying you. My child you are in complete control of this creative process. What if you altered your perspective to see that which you are creating now to that which you desire to experience? For as you purchase your lottery tickets every week or enter that home or car giveaway drawing every day in hopes of feeling special, ask yourself what you desire to experience. As you enter your name are you envisioning having this material possession from your eyes of truth or from the perspective of fear?

In other words if you desire to win abundance of wealth, are you envisioning how the world perceives you while driving your brand new luxury car or are you experiencing this as the creator? When you envision the media attention, are you drawing energy from taking the attention in order to feel special and validated, or are you perceiving this attention as an unnecessary distraction? When you visualize spending your new found fortune, are you experiencing first-hand the feelings of joy or are you having emotions of arrogance and pride as you envision your family and friends envy? How you perceive your experience on a greater level will allow you to understand your true intentions in the act of creation.

If you are not connected on a soul level to that which you desire to experience my child, you will not have the experience of creating it. Love creates love and joy creates more joy. Yet fear, envy, and a sense of false pride are all emotions used in the manifestation process as well. The problem so often arises when you desire to win a special fortune that another has created. Rather than seeing the opportunity for you to create the same fortune through your own power, you choose to view this as the only way to have fortune. So many of you have convinced yourself that you can never have abundance of joy, love, or money. As a result, you seek the expression of these things in the world outside of you. Only you cannot take that which is not yours to have, so rather than allowing yourself to be inspired into creating these for yourself, you choose to compete for it outside of self.

The lottery as you know it is an illusion my child, as it represents a chance to win a coveted prize if only you do something for it. Yet I ask you, how can you win something that you already possess within you? For if you are all connected to your Source energy through the power of all that is, then how can you be separate of that which you desire except but of your perception of that separateness? You have been taught an illusion from your inception that you are somehow separate from those souls and things around you. This illusion has prevented you from seeing truth through the eyes of God. For I ask you again, how can you be separate from that which is already connected to you? Cease from seeing the world outside of you as a separate entity, but instead choose to perceive everything as a part of the greater whole. By doing this, you enter into reality and into the truth that you can have any experience your heart desires to create.

Are you prepared to own this truth, even if it is for a moment? Can you allow yourself to no longer live in your own deception but to acknowledge what your heart and soul already know? For you write these words as the author and the creator of your experience. You are telling the story of that which is already created but is yet to be seen. Since you are the creator of your own story, you write it out word for word from the beginning through the words on the pages of your books. These books which have all shared your answered prayer in the form of words, of my words. Yet you also chose to honor your purpose of creating the connection through story of the truth that you are all one, and connected to each other both in life and in the spirit form. My child, you knew of your goal to share with another soul that which you know to be truth.

You are all one and will forever be one with your Creator and with one another. There is no experience you cannot create out of thought, emotion, and action other than by choice. Yet you understood this on such a soul level that you chose to experience the creation of that which the world outside of you would consider to be a miracle, and document this in order for all to understand. The lottery is no more a game of luck than your moments of creation in life. In order to experience the "prize" you must identify that which you desire to have in your life. Whether it be abundance of love, joy, peace of mind, or money, you choose the prize through your own standards. The "chance" of you getting this prize is determined by the power of your own hand. Your thoughts and emotions create the experience of having that which you desire.

You need not see it in the world outside of you in order to experience its presence in the world within you. For you must first create that connection by seeking that which is seeking you and align your energy to it in order to receive. The consideration is the action you take in order to bring that very thing which you desire into your life. Seek not to understand the creative process as just entering your name into a drawing with millions of other souls who desire the same experience and think this is all you must do to create your experience. If you consider that entering a drawing takes but a moment of your time and minimal focus of energy, then how can you believe you will have that which you desire?

As a co-creator in your own life, you must focus your energy and align your thoughts, emotions, and actions into creating the experience before you witness its inception in the world outside of you. No longer convince yourself of an illusion that I seek not to validate you through giving you all that you desire my child. For when you realize it is you who must validate self in order to be a creator in your own life, then you will empower yourself in ways you never imagined. This is your purpose. To share it with the world and allow even one soul to see their own truth through the connection of this truth. For I have been sending you messengers of light and truth throughout time. Souls are being awakened and following their calling by creating the life they desire to experience in love and joy. Be that joy and always remember you are the essence of my love.

Lesson Twenty Eight
WRITE YOUR STORY

"Be still and know that by sharing your gift and your story, some will relate to the experience of knowing their soul and learning to trust in their power of prayer. Through these pages and through the love from these words, the truth will be the message. You are called to deliver that truth to another who will learn from it, and seek their own through prayer."

Excerpt from Through the Eyes of Truth: A Conversation with God about My Life, Your Life, and Discovering Our Purpose

Many souls have adopted the illusion that I answer the prayers to only those whom I selectively seek to connect with. This illusion has separated many souls from me, not realizing they are already one with their Creator. Yet rather than seek to change their perspective, they alter their standards and settle for a life not worthy of them. How can you be so willing to adopt a false belief before you choose to seek truth from within? Although you are taught from a young age that the love of God must be earned, your spirit still seeks truth from the walls of your soul. Yet rather than spend moments of contemplation on understanding the truth of your soul, you choose to adopt negative illusions that separate you from experiencing a relationship with me.

My child there has never been an unanswered prayer. Yet you choose to believe the illusion that I hear you not. Since you are fully in control of your own thoughts, then there cannot be another soul who forces you to believe in an illusion. You are in control of what you think and how you choose to feel, so you are in fact controlling your own path. Understanding this, how can you honestly blame God for not granting you communion when you control your own experiences? The reason you feel not the connection and bond between me and your own heart, is because you have spent countless years ignoring my whispers into your soul.

I hear every prayer called out to me in silence and through the cries of your soul. I know every thought you have, and answer you through the channels of thought that you know so well. I feel your soul when you have no words to express the depths of your raw emotion. Do you not believe for a moment that I hear not that which I am? Do you dare to ignore my answered prayer to you when I wrap my loving arms around each and every one of you? How can you believe that you are a child of God yet fear that I hear you not, nor know your cries? There is an illusion that is creating a blanket of fear across the souls of this journey. This illusion being that you are all separate from me and I am separate from you. Your soul knows on such a deep level this false belief is stemmed from fear, yet you choose not to honor that light shining truth from your spirit.

It is as if you are punishing yourself for being less than perfect and believe you are not worthy of my love. I have shouted to you that I love you unconditionally through the depths of your soul and you hear me not. I have moved mountains and parted seas to reveal to you the depth of my power and majesty only to have this met with more deceit. It is as if you are so angry at yourself that you refuse to acknowledge your own connection to me. Yet in your despair you still cry out to me. How can you think yourself of not being worthy enough for my love yet when I extend it to you, you receive it not? My child you have become so intertwined in a ball of illusion, you are struggling to free yourself from the web of deceit. Yet you find yourself not worthy enough to realize you are not restrained.

My love for you reaches beyond the depths of the greatest oceans and past the light of a million galaxies. There is nothing you can do to ever separate my love from you, for you and I are one. Together we reside in the same cell of life and creation. Do you not see that in your struggle to find yourself, you have denied me as well? Because of this, I send you messengers who have also struggled with your fear. These messengers have experienced the overwhelming despair and agony that you have, so they chose to honor their calling to remind you of yours. Yet you often witness these messengers of love and call them lucky among you rather than realizing I sent them to you as reminders that you are never alone. Since I have not received your attention, then I send you another who has chosen to impart her journey so you too may uncover your own.

This messenger is not chosen from worth rather from obedience. For the act of answering your God call in the darkest moments of your life, allow you to journey through the roads of deception into the valley of truth. The fear you experience is only a perception, and when you choose to change your perception then you alter your course through your journey. How many times have you heard the echo of my whispers into your soul yet ignored them as only your imagination. Yet you pray to me within the silence of your mind and ask for dreams that only your imagination can create. How else would I honor your prayer to me my child, than to reach you through the vessel which you sent to me? If you call out to me in the still of your mind, I will answer your prayer in the still of your mind.

If you reach out to me in prayer through your words, will I not respond to you through the manner in which you sent forth your prayer? For I seek only to connect with you in the manner which you desire to experience. Yet when you hear my voice resonating through the walls of your soul, you choose to ignore me rather than tune into me. You fear not only your own greatness in who you are but in what you are capable of creating. So then it becomes easier for you to turn your back to that which you seek in order not to answer your own call. You then take this illusion one step further and dare blame me for saying "no," when in fact you are the creator of your own experience and said no to your God.

As a co-creator in your life do you not realize that your journey is not to create in fear, but to own your power as a child of God and create love and joy in your life? For when I answer your prayer I will seek conversation and communion with you. Your voice is my voice and your hands are my hands. Your heart seeks to know oneness with me and your soul longs to hear the echo of my whisper throughout its entirety. For when you seek me with all of your heart you will hear my words as your truth. Only this time it will be my answer you heed when the world outside of you is creating more illusions. You will know my voice within you so clearly that you will understand what it is to be in communion with the Divine.

Only then will I ask you to create your journey in the loving manner which fills your soul with more joy and love. I will call upon you as a reminder that you are the creator and the observer in the story of your own life. Your words will inspire the memory of who you are before you came into this illusion filled journey. Suddenly your transformation will create the bond of togetherness you have sought for all of these years. For you must change something within your course in order to have a different outcome in your experience. I will guide you through the change, as it will be my words you hear and my calling you answer in the still of the night. There will be no other message resonating within you other than the truth of my words shining a light within your soul. This light will reveal the path of the unknown as you journey through a soul journey all your own.

As you document the expression of love and joy from your soul, you will do so in the manner which is most familiar to you and brings you the most fulfillment. For as a powerful creator in your own journey through life, you create through the same channels that I have created all there is. The word is a powerful vehicle of truth and you will honor the words resonating within the walls of your soul, and transform them into the written word for which to share your story. At first this story will appear to be a small figment of your own imagination from where you shared your deepest prayer with me. Then as you write my words of truth in the story of your life, you will realize this is just a part of the greater whole in the book of life.

Within every story lies a journey through trials and tribulations that other souls are experiencing. This story is just a reminder to every soul who will read it, that they too are connected as one to each other and as one to God. One thought, one power, one Source. Yet as the truth of this story unfolds, you will reveal through the chapters of a magical journey through the crossroads of life. The overall message of this book will remind many that they are not alone. In a world where few choose to see one another on the streets and through the rooms of life, you will remind them that the eyes are in fact the windows to the soul.

You walk among a world where it is now more acceptable to stare at a computer or telephone screen. You teach your children it is more important to play games or watch videos than it is to connect your eyes to the world around you. Not to be inundated with fear and illusion, but to remind one another that you are all one. You awaken in the mornings and reach for your technology escapes before you reach for your Creator and wonder why you feel alone. Your children witness you build relationships with a computer and yet you wonder why they fail to look you in the eyes and speak truth. Where are your eyes throughout your life? Are they fixated on a computer screen or are they acknowledging the value of human life?

Then you take this illusion further and judge your Creator as you judge yourself. For if you find not one another worthy of connecting and inspiring then why would your God find you worthy? You then dig a deeper trench of illusion in which to escape and create the cycle once again. Only when you ask in prayer for that which you desire do you seek to have communion with me. When I seek to answer you, then you have already removed your attention from prayer to technology and seek the answers from the world outside of you. The same world who is seeking validation outside of themselves and experiencing the same fears of feeling lost and isolated. My child you have created such a pattern of this cycle, that you have convinced yourself it is reality. Change your perception and choose to view life through the eyes of possibilities, and you will create what the world deems as the impossible.

What if you honor those around you by honoring your soul calling? When you look into a computer screen, allow it to advance your purpose rather than prevent you from discovering it. What if you could write one chapter in the book of life with your own contribution to love and prayer? What would you say? How would you want to impact the world around you which is in fact one within you? For when I call upon you to write your story in the book of life, I seek not to reveal to you the final book in advance. On the contrary, I will ask for your chapter and only whisper into your soul the outcome of the book without proof of its existence. Only then will you be called upon to trust the outcome and contribute what your soul desires to share in love.

My child this book is just one chapter in the story of your life. As you write it out word for word, you are in fact creating the connection to that which is in the spiritual realm and that which is in the physical realm. Your faith will lead you through the darkest corners of your illusion and reveal light in the realm of truth. For I wish not to control your experiences, rather to guide you back into the truth of your own creative power and the connection that you are one with me and I with you. There has never been a moment in time when we were not connected, yet your illusion through this physical journey has created the perception of separateness. Yet it doesn't have to define you. Use this as an inner beacon that you must alter your course back into reality once again.

What better way to reveal this truth to you than through the power of a beautiful story. One that will ignite the light in another soul to remember their own truth. Yet this story has been revealed in order for you to understand that every soul walking through this journey of life is connected one to another. This story is to remind every soul of the power they have to create the life of their dreams and to understand that nothing is impossible in the spiritual realm. The only requirements are to walk in faith and to hear my voice. Yet in this journey you will receive unlimited love and joy from experiencing your own gifts through the power of creation. You will remind others they too have the same connection to the Divine as you have, and I am only waiting to help them write their own chapter of their story in the book of their life.

You need not see the end from the beginning. Only trust that I am that which I am. I have led you through the green pastures only to reveal to you a world so filled with joy, you will know not where I end and you begin. Have faith in the communion of prayer and know it is an honor when you include me in on your journey. Seek not that which no longer serves you, but know you alone must walk your path into truth with only the sound of my voice whispering throughout your soul. I will guide you and lead you into a truth so profound that you will one day see your life as one with everyone and everything around you. Know that I do not call upon those who hear not my voice, but those who are listening and honoring the quiet whispers in their soul. Seek me and know I am that I am.

Lesson Twenty Nine
THE LOTTERY ILLUSION

"So when you turn on the news and discover that another lucky soul has won wealth beyond their expectations, understand the person who is experiencing winning the lottery is the person who already understood on a soul level they were going to win. This is just as powerful as the boy who is staying up late studying his math to become a teacher, or the young teenage girl who is practicing her lab study to get into medical school. The same can be said for the talented athlete who was born into a family with very little money yet possesses great love for their talent, and will someday light up the court with a professional team endorsement. These souls all won the "lottery" in their own right. For their purpose was to experience what their soul truly loved, and in the process became very successful and abundant."

Excerpt from Through the Eyes of Truth: A Conversation with God about My Life, Your Life, and Discovering Our Purpose

This day as you write these words the lottery is at the highest value in its history. The world has awakened to the possibility that somewhere, a lucky soul will experience sudden abundance of wealth. Yet how many of these souls who are buying a ticket are also creating their own world of abundance in all that they seek to experience? Somehow you believe that winning a lottery is the only way to experience large amounts of money. Yet when you pray to me for wealth, for a new home, a new car... do you not seek for your Source to answer and provide you with these items? How is it that you can value the lottery illusion greater than you value reality in the world of possibilities where you reside? You seek that which is outside of you and believe your chances of experiencing wealth beyond measure will be yours, yet choose to avoid having a relationship with your God who is guaranteed to answer your prayers and lead you to your own truth.

I have awakened souls across the world to the possibility of all that is through this lucky game so many of you are playing. Yet rather than seek Source to continue in the creation of your dreams, many of you will close your eyes to the truth of your own potential immediately after the lucky numbers are drawn and fall back into your slumber of sorrow and hopelessness. Do you not believe for a moment that you too can create abundance of all you desire through your own power? My child you have fallen into a well of deception so deep, you have grown more comfortable in the emotions of mediocrity than allowing yourself to experience love in all you can create. For I seek not to tease you by drawing you near to the possibilities of endless wealth only to close the doors on that wealth in your life. I seek only to connect you to the power that lies within you.

Yet as co-creators of your own experiences, you choose to close the doors to the reality of oneness with me, and live in a trance that allows you not the courage to explore the unknown corners of your mind. For every soul has the possibility of creating wealth in every area of your life, yet you choose to believe in limits and lack. You would rather allow the dream of winning a lottery to temporarily affect your dream state than awaken to the wonder that you too can create anything you desire your own life.

So many of you believe that owning millions of dollars will somehow remove the pain in your heart from experiences past. You would rather rely on building blocks of illusion than to step out into oneness with your Creator. Do you not understand that although you seek temporary comfort from your own life experiences, it is not money that you seek? Wealth is as much an illusion as is the lie you convince yourself of that you are not worthy of having all you desire. For the soul who created this wealth has done so with the intention to awaken you out of your sleep-like state of mind. Maybe their intention was to remind you of your own ability to create what the world deems impossible. What if a group of souls created the largest jackpot in the world to shake you out of your slumber and help you remember what you are capable of? For as quickly as the drawing will take place, many of you will slide back into your trance and forget there was ever the possibility of "what if."

You lay awake at night dreaming of how you would spend your money and ask yourself, what you would do if you won this jackpot prize. Will you walk through the doors of this new reality and envision yourself giving away money to relatives, friends, and even strangers? The thought of this brings temporary joy to your soul as you believe money is the answer to all of life's problems. What you fail to realize my child is the soul you are ultimately attempting to bring joy to, is your own. For you know not how another soul experiences their lives, so you cannot understand what emotions providing them financial support will provide. You must first create the abundance in your own life only to understand how to remind another what they must do to create abundance in their lives.

For it is not the teachers' job to support the student. Instead it becomes the role of the teacher to remind the student of how they too can tap into their own unlimited potential and create the life of their dream. Wealth provides no more peace and abundance of love in a soul's life than not having that wealth will bring. As you know not how another soul processes their own dreams and ability to love themselves, so you cannot understand how to fix them in the illusion of life. You must first awaken to the love you tap into through the power of God, and grow the connection within yourself to witness the world outside of yourself change. For some this change will be instant and for others it may take more energy, but you will all reach a place where you can create your own utopia with or without there ever being a perceived lottery experience.

The greatest illusion is that you must seek your abundance of all you desire outside of yourself. All you ever need to create the experiences you seek in joy can be obtained by tapping into the Source of all there is within you. Yet rather than take the time to understand who you are and what you are capable of, many of you would rather spend that time convincing another of your own illusion. How many of you enter into drawings or sweepstakes only to spend your thought and energy convincing another soul the ultimate prize is yours to claim? Do you not understand the soul who has already created the experience you see manifested in the physical world is the only soul who can claim that which is theirs? Somehow you convince yourself the illusion that you have the right to inherit another soul's dream once you see it manifested before you. I tell you this. No soul can claim the lottery of life unless the soul who has created it releases it to another.

When you realize you had not the right to claim that which another created, you blame your God for not finding you worthy enough. The truth is my child, you found yourself not worthy enough. Otherwise you would have been the soul to create this and touched your heart upon every detail in the creative process. Rather than looking at this prize as a goal to own, you would have recognized it from your soul that it was seeking you as well. There is a recognition when you realize a dream fulfilled, that the dreamer and the dream are in fact one and the same. There is no separation of one from another but through the experience of creation and receiving. Do you understand this my child? For when you know from the truth of who you are as one with your Creator, you will understand that dream which you seek is seeking you as well.

Honor your creative gifts and cease from living in an illusion that you must seek something outside of yourself in order to be complete. I am one with you and am experiencing all that I am through the expression of you. Align yourself with truth and know you have all you need through the power of God to experience what the world would consider a miracle. Rather than seeking to duplicate another's expression of self, choose to be authentic and create your own. Because one or many souls seek to create one way of creating abundance does not mean you must mimic their course. It merely reminds you that through free will, you can create a course of your own which is filled with magical moments between you and your God.

Lesson Thirty
STAY THE COURSE

"This world is filled with dreamers who have chosen to relinquish their power to create dreams and have become unbelievers because they choose not to have faith. If you have faith in God then you must complete the process by believing in yourself. For God cannot open a door that through free will, you choose not to place your hand upon. You are co-creators, which means that you need one another to complete the process of creation."

Excerpt from Heaven Scent:
Love Letters from Beyond

Do you now understand that you are already one with the dream you seek? For when you are able to understand this truth on a soul level, you will achieve mastery upon realizing you are not your conditions. At any point in your evolution you will know you can change your thoughts to alter your course. Yet how many souls will travel through the veil of light only wishing they had understood this truth and experienced it on a greater level in their lives? There are so many souls my child who are experience the broken dreams of their lives and placing the burden on their lack of worthiness? They have convinced themselves they are the experience they failed to accomplish, so they associate themselves as failure.

When you awaken to the truth that failure is as much an illusion as is fear, then you will understand the greatness of who you are. Yet rather than dismiss the emotions and thoughts of failure, so many souls choose to identify with those emotions of fear and disappointment, thus they cannot separate themselves from the feelings. This in turn creates the unity of the emotions of disappointment. The feelings become so overwhelming that it consumes the soul until they cannot separate their own soul from their feelings. Because of this, it becomes more difficult to bear the burden of disappointment and they make a conscious decision not to add to those emotions, so they disconnect from self and thus from their God.

For if you are one with me and create your life through the awareness of me, then you have only fear to create when you are no longer aware of my presence within you. Rather than seek to know yourself through love in the arms of all that is love, you detach from me and live your life in fear. I have called many to awaken the hearts of those who still seek to know self through their Creator. Some will awaken and answer the call while others will remain in their fear based trance. What will you do my child, when it is time to answer the call to awaken the souls in the world around you one person at a time? Will you cease to know self because you feel not worthy enough, or will you answer my call?

Be prepared to answer your own call through the truth of these words as they resonate within the walls of your soul. Know that you are aligned with your higher purpose, and have only to choose to connect with my light to guide you through the waters of life. You know truth as it resonates through your heart, yet you fear your own greatness. Being in alignment to receive is as important as aligning to recognize that which you are creating my child. For if you choose not to receive your creation, then how can you share with those souls around you the tools of remembering who they are? Do you not understand you must first walk your path alone so you may share with those who are lonely how to connect with their Creator?

Seek not the advice nor the approval from the world around you. Close your ears to those who shout illusion from the walls of their fear. They seek not to hinder you but to claim that which is not theirs. You have only to hear my voice and seek my truth in order to find your greatest blessings lying waiting for you among green pastures. If you falter in your faith and choose not to answer the call before manifesting your vision, then how can that dream you desire to create be seen? For I call forth not those who are standing boasting through their pride. Instead I call the meek who seek to know truth before deceit, and honor me before they honor themselves.

You come from a world where recognition is the God you seek, yet when you receive this burden of being known then the world calls you forth into judgment. Rather than embrace you, they choose to see their faults through you. Many have walked away from their calling out of fear of being placed in a mirror that reflects the emotions of those around them. For you cannot understand that which another seeks to know of themselves, but only to serve as a mirror to reflect back to another their own thoughts and emotions. This seems so simple yet is a greater cross to bear. How can you separate the voice of God from man when the voices of those around you scream louder into your ears than does your Source? By tapping into truth and into the whisper of my words resonating through the walls of your soul, and knowing that I am that I am.

My child, your words will create the awareness of this burden being dismissed by so many and heard by the courageous few. For when you are called upon to remind the world of their bliss that awaits them through the connection of their soul, you must walk this path alone. How can you listen to the voices of those around you and heed your guidance through me? You have to serve but one God, and cannot heed the voices of man when I am guiding you into truth. For many will embark upon their own journey after reading these words, and will sing to the song of their own soul without the awareness from another. They too will understand the sound of humility resonating through the walls of their soul when I whisper into their soul and call them to their own purpose.

Fear not, for I know your fears and am awakening you to the love of your own life calling. You have nothing to seek outside of you, as Source resides within you. Be aware and be diligent in your own persistent journey into self. The closer you become to awakening the louder the sounds echoing from the voice of fear outside of you will ring. For theirs is not to take that which is already created by another. Only to be reminded they too have the power to manifest their hearts true desire from the power of love and through the power of God. Go forth and know you have answered your call. Your words will resonate through the walls of many souls that meet them. For many have been awakened to the sound of their own truth only to discover fear has clouded their path.

They will understand they need not be perfect in their journey, as they are already perfection in all they are. These souls will know from the depths of their heart I judge them not, but instead embrace them and call them to meet me in communion. Fear not that which you seek is beyond your grasp. As you are a powerful co-creator in your experience of life and have all the tools you need to bring an abundance of love, joy, and peace into your reality. You need only be aware of the power you have to create abundance in all areas of your life, and allow Source to guide you back to your truth. I am with you always and have been one with you since your inception through me. For we are never apart. Only your perception of separateness makes you perceive being incomplete.

Are you willing to release old patterns of thought and action and replace them with your truth? Now go forth and know all that I have stated is come to pass. You need not fear from when this will manifest itself before you. What you must be aware of is doing that which brings love and joy into your heart. Then the souls who will connect with you will also connect with their own love and joy. As I have reminded you that you serve as a mirror and not as the salvation. Let your words resonate from the corners of your soul and allow your story to guide others to their truth. For I seek to remind every soul they are one with their Creator and one with another. Nothing can remove the everlasting love I have for every soul who has ever been. I judge not, but remove judgment from you when connected as one with you.

Your course is set and you will share in these words. Know the time is near and fast approaching for you to become that which your heart has always desired to be. Go forth in the stillness of the night and light the heart of souls you meet one heartbeat at a time. You need not recognize them, for your words will reach those who are meant to discover their truth at this moment. I have created a blanket of love to cover the hearts of the weary and the souls of my children. No longer allow another to instruct you as to what to think, rather remember for yourselves *how* to think. You need not an instruction manual for living, as so many of you are walking your path and slowly dying from loneliness and fear one moment after another.

For your life journey was not about living in fear but creating your experiences through your moments of love. Stop seeking that which brings you more into an illusion of fear, but know that you too will all awaken from your slumber and become complete with me once again. Meanwhile, cherish your moments of life and surround your hearts and your home with joy and love. There is nothing to prove to another. Cherish yourselves as you cherish those around you. Honor yourself as you honor those outside of you. Cease from seeking perfection in one another and embrace every soul as being an extension of you. As you are all extensions of me, and I am one with you now and forever. I need only to remind you of our completeness to make your journey more enjoyable.

Life is but a playground so seek to experience joy within yourself first. Only then will you know what it is to be the magnificent children of God you are. I need nothing from you in order to love and know myself. There is nothing you can do to disobey me, for I seek not perfection from you. How can I seek to condemn that which I am? I seek only to remind each soul who connects with even one word in these messages, that you are loved beyond measure. If I create what the world deems as a miracle in order to remind you that you and I are one, then the miracle was not for the chosen but for all of my chosen children. For I have carefully selected the creation of all that is in order to know myself through you. Each soul walking the journey through life has been called and chosen for the experience of perfection. Enjoy your journey and know you are worthy beyond what you can comprehend. Allow me to show you a world where you and I are one in mind, body, and soul. Do I have your attention now? Have I described even one magical moment that has brought you closer to me?

For I call you throughout every moment of your existence to awaken and hear my voice. Reach out to me in prayer and seek communion with me. This experience you are participating in was created for you and by you. To be reminded of your connection to your God. There are no coincidences, although many will read these words and attempt to convince you that you are not the chosen soul they were meant for. Yet you will be reminded through one word, one thought, and one feeling that sparks within you a very special journey into your truth. Awaken my child and leave your bags at the front door of your old journey. Open your heart and your mind to the miracles that lay within you. Know that where truth is love resides. This precious journey was not about a house or material possessions. This was about discovering your own home within the walls of your soul.

Yet I used a group of souls who all answered their own call in the still of the night. These souls did not seek one another to write their chapter in the book of this creation. They merely answered their call to awakening and chose to walk their path without the approval or the permission from another. As their journey made way through paths of excitement, sorrow, and ultimately joy, they found one another and discovered they were all a part of the story. One that was written specifically for you in order to awaken you to live your destiny in the book of life. For had you been looking only at the outcome of what you thought was the prize, you would have missed the story. The magical awakening was to remind you that you are a precious child of God. Nothing will ever separate my love from you. I am one with you and you are one with me. I needed only to remind you of your own perfection. Are you listening? Have I gotten your attention? Now pick up your pen and write your story in the book of life. I love you now and forever.

"Go in peace and share the knowledge of this truth with those souls who are ready to discover their truth. I have created them to become that which they have always desired to be. Seek me first, and I will guide you through the waters of life. I will instill within your hearts that which shall become untouchable. When the world looks into your eyes, they will see only truth. Only then will they discover their prayers were always heard, their cries have been my cries, and the journey into their own truth will begin with their realization that they have always been perfect in my eyes. When you cry out to me and seek me with all your heart, you will discover your truth, your voice, and your majesty waiting for you in the still of the night. Bow your head now and know that every prayer is felt, heard, and acknowledged. I hear your thoughts, I know your voice, and I feel your cries. For you are all a child of God, and have been born into inheriting all that you love, in order to experience love to the fullest in this lifetime. Pray to me child, and I will hear you. There is never a lost voice, or a silent cry, as I hear all of my precious children when you call out to me in the still of the night, praying "Hosanna in the highest, have mercy on me, and hear my prayer."

Excerpt from Through the Eyes of Truth:
A Conversation with God about My Life, Your Life, and Discovering Our Purpose

Live Inspired Miracle Worker!

Other Books by Suzy Bootz

Through the Eyes of Truth – A Conversation with God about My Life, Your Life, and Discovering Our Purpose: Audio book available on Audible, and Print on Amazon

Heaven Scent – Love Letters from Beyond: Available on Amazon

Creating Utopia – Living Life as a Miracle Worker: Available on Amazon

Follow Us On:

Twitter: @realsuzybootz

Instagram: @realsuzybootz

To live inspired please visit www.suzybootz.com

www.ingramcontent.com/pod-product-compliance
Lightning Source LLC
Chambersburg PA
CBHW070548160426
43199CB00014B/2418